MW01698361

THE LONG-EXPECTED JESUS

Also by Rick Thompson

Radical Growth

How the Agrarian Models of the New Testament
Lead to Spiritual Maturity

THE LONG-EXPECTED JESUS

How the Old Testament Reveals the Eternal Son of God

Rick Thompson

Family Advent Devotionals by Heather McAnear

Unless otherwise noted, all Scripture quotations are taken from the The Holy Bible, New International Version®, NIV® Copyright © 1973, 1978, 1984, 2011 by Biblica, Inc.® Used by permission. All rights reserved worldwide.

Published by Council Road Baptist Church
2900 N. Council Road
Bethany, OK 73008

www.councilroad.org

Author: Rick Thompson
Family Bible Study Author: Heather McAnear
Editor: Sarah Sutton
Layout and Cover Design: Brad Mardis

All illustrations by Gustave Doré are public domain.

ALL RIGHTS RESERVED
No portion of this book may be reproduced in any form, except for brief quotations in reviews, without written permission from the publisher.

For

Teri, Taylor, Tallie and Ailee

Contents

Acknowledgements

This project would not have been close to complete if it had not been for the hard work and dedication of some very important people in my life. I am truly grateful for my assistant, editor and good friend Sarah Sutton for her countless hours of correcting, proofing and generally "cleaning up" the manuscript. Also, for the excellent graphic design and set up by Brad Mardis who went beyond mere artistic design and actually read the manuscript and then put his heart into it. I am also indebted to my friends Curtis Brown and Todd Tamura who read the manuscript and provided invaluable input and to my friend Mike Romero who first gave me the idea for this book and was a huge encouragement as it was written. I am also especially thankful for the good work of Heather McAnear in developing the family devotions. And finally, my wife Teri, who as always is my strong support and grounding and who sacrificed greatly to help get me through this project.

Introduction

In the summer of 2014, I had the privilege of spending two weeks at Tyndale House in Cambridge on a study leave. It was there that this book was written. I don't know that I have ever been to a place that so inspired research and edifying fellowship. I very much enjoyed my conversations with PhD students, professors, and other scholars from around the world who had converged on that place for the purpose of research. All of them were devoted Christians who had committed their lives to the world of academics. I am forever indebted to Dr. Peter Williams and all of the excellent staff at Tyndale House for their hospitality. It is wonderful to know that such a place exists at a leading world university.

The many colleges at Cambridge have a history that is almost impossible to believe. It is the university that inspired people such as Sir Isaac Newton, William Tyndale, Erasmus, William Wilberforce, C.S. Lewis, and Malcolm Mugeridge. Truly it is a city that has shaped world history through the disciplines of religion, politics, biology, genetics, and the list goes on. On our next to the last day at Cambridge, Teri and I spent a wonderful day with Wayne and Margaret Grudem. Dr. Wayne Grudem is the author of several books on theology and ethics and has been coming to Tyndale House since he first earned a PhD at Cambridge over forty years ago. I made the observation to Wayne that I had felt real inspiration while working on this book at Cambridge. He replied, "I believe God has His hand on this place. There is nothing like it on Earth." After my time there, I would have to agree.

In my research for this book, I read many other books that deal with the topic of Christ in the Old Testament. I am especially indebted to the fine work David Murray did in his book, *Jesus on Every Page*, Christopher Wright's book, *Knowing Jesus Through the Old Testament*, and the series of lectures by F.F. Bruce on the subject. One of the things I noticed in all the reading I have done is that while most books tend to focus on the New Testament usage of Old Testament passages or Old Testament prophecies fulfilled in the New Testament, not much was written about how the variety of images, foreshadowing, and prophecies together built toward the first Advent. I am hoping that this book can accomplish that on some level. That said, it is certainly not meant to be a scholarly work on the subject, but rather for inspirational reading.

I am a pastor through and through. And so the pages you are about to read are the writings of a pastor to his congregation about the subject, "How the Old Testament points us to Christ." I prepared this book with the idea of preaching a series of sermons on the subject matter later in the year.

It is intended to be read during the Advent season, with every chapter serving as a devotional for each of the twenty-five days of Advent. From the first page to the last, I thought of my wonderful congregation at Council Road Baptist Church, whose love and support for me through the years I certainly have not deserved, but who have blessed me and my family beyond words.

THE LONG-EXPECTED JESUS

PART ONE
Expectation

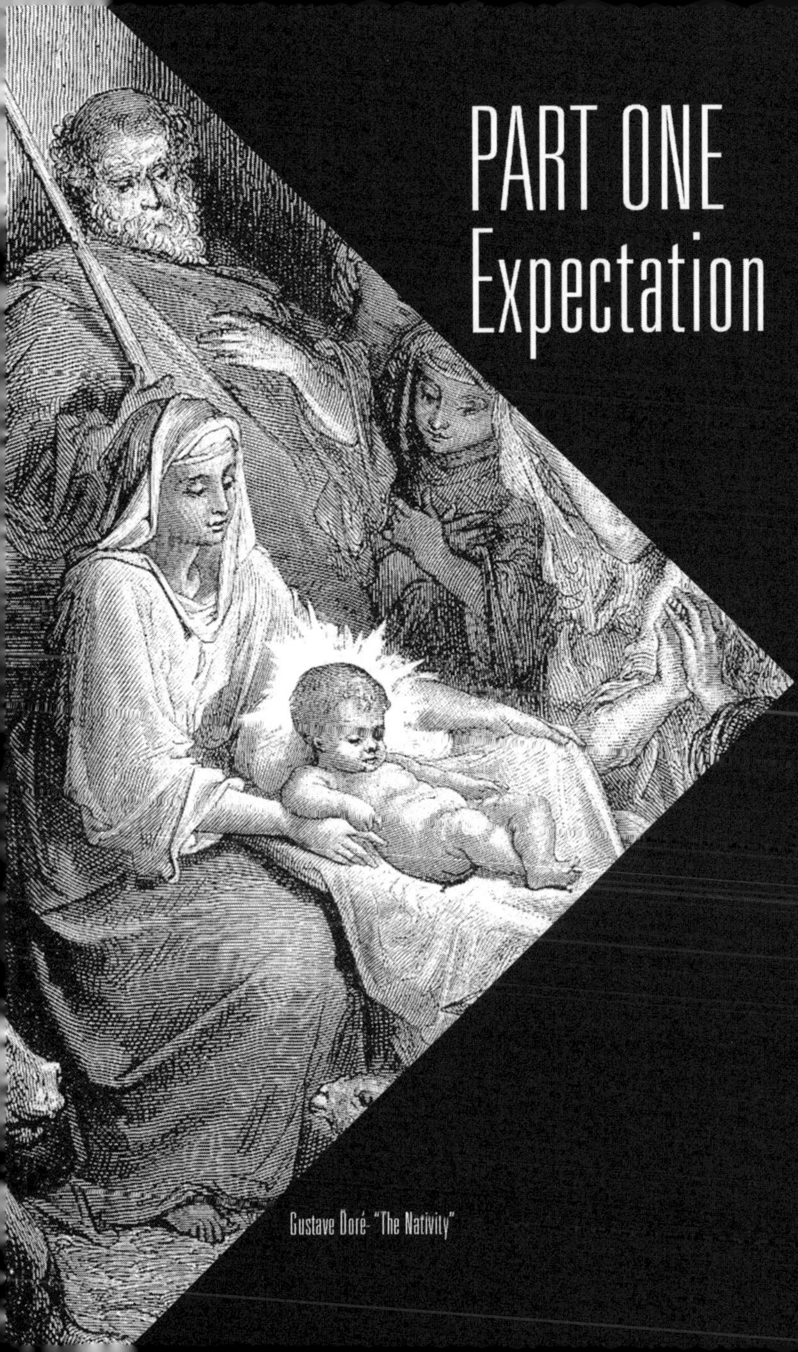

Gustave Doré- "The Nativity"

One: We've Been Expecting You

His mercy extends to those who fear him,
from generation to generation.
He has performed mighty deeds with his arm;
he has scattered those who are proud in their inmost thoughts.
He has brought down rulers from their thrones
but has lifted up the humble.
He has filled the hungry with good things
but has sent the rich away empty.
He has helped his servant Israel,
remembering to be merciful
to Abraham and his descendants forever,
just as he promised our ancestors
(Luke 1:50-55).

As I look back at my life, I can think of moments in time that have the greatest significance and clarity. I remember like it was yesterday when my wife and I first learned that she was pregnant with our first child. It all seemed so surreal, so exciting and yet scary all at the same time. I was a relatively young man, and she was even younger, and we both felt somewhat overwhelmed by the weight of responsibility. Were we really prepared for this journey ahead? It seemed as if in that moment something significant and powerful had changed in us. Of course, the biggest change would be in Teri, as she was carrying a new life inside her, but at the same time I was carrying something as well. As strange as it may seem, when I first heard the news from

Teri, I could immediately feel myself changing with her. I was not carrying a baby, but I was carrying a new responsibility as a man who would support and take care of my wife and growing family. Together, we would prepare for the coming of this child and plan out our lives ahead. We began to prepare a room in our home, and friends and family rallied around us.

The weeks and months ahead were filled with anticipation and expectation. Would the baby be a boy or girl? What would he or she look like? Would the baby have blond hair like Teri or brown hair like me? Brown eyes or blue? Olive skin or freckles? Teri and I would speculate about everything from the baby's size and shape to personality type, intellect, and athletic ability. We obsessed over the details of taking care of a baby. Baby showers reaped an abundant harvest of baby blankets, clothes, toys, and diapers. I remember the day the doctor looked at the sonogram and told us that our baby was a boy. How our hearts flooded with anticipation at the news! To say that we were "expectant parents" was an understatement!

What is true for expectant parents obsessing over every detail of the coming of a child can also be said of the coming of Jesus. But more than the joy and anticipation of Joseph and Mary, Jesus was anticipated on a much grander scale. Jesus was anticipated from the beginning of time itself to be the One who would bring about God's redemptive plan for all of mankind.

What we will see in the pages ahead is that like obsessive parents preparing and anticipating the coming of a child, the ancient script written in ages past by the patriarchs, poets, and prophets of the Old Testament pointed to the coming of the Anointed One. Truly, He was the long-expected Messiah, and the anticipation of His coming was written on every page.

The Christmas hymn that inspired the title of this book was written in 1835 by Charles Wesley and aptly expresses that point in this way:

Come, O long-expected Jesus,
Born to set your people free;
From our fears and sins release us
By your death on Calvary.

Israel's strength and consolation,
Hope to all the earth impart,
dear desire of ev'ry nation,
Joy of ev'ry longing heart.
Born your people to deliver,
Born a child and yet a king;
Born to reign in us forever,
Now your gracious kingdom bring.

By your own eternal Spirit
Rule in all our hearts alone;
By your all-sufficient merit
Raise us to your glorious throne.

Reflect:

Luke 1:50-55 is a part of the song of Mary known as the "magnificat." Read the entire song in Luke 1:46-55. What do you believe it means when it says, "He has helped his servant Israel in remembrance of his mercy, as he spoke to our fathers, to Abraham and to his offspring forever"? Why is it significant that these words were spoken in the context of her immaculate conception? In what ways do you believe Jesus was expected for generations before His birth?

Two: Your Concept of Jesus May Be Too Small

When I was a child, I talked like a child, I thought like a child, I reasoned like a child. When I became a man, I put the ways of childhood behind me. For now we see only a reflection as in a mirror; then we shall see face to face. Now I know in part; then I shall know fully, even as I am fully known (1 Corinthians 13:10-12).

Many years ago when I was a pastor in Texas, a young mother came up to me after one of our Christmas Eve services and told me about a conversation she had with her six-year-old daughter the previous week.

The local college in town put on an amazing drive-through Christmas display each year featuring thousands of Christmas lights and decorations. It also included the Texas version of live nativity farm animals—cows, donkeys, sheep and goats, as well as a Shetland pony or two and at least one year a few Pygmy pigs. And of course, they also featured actors portraying Mary and Joseph sitting in a lean-to barn with a baby in "swaddling cloths" lying in a manger. The display was immensely popular, especially among families with small children.

This young family from our church made the drive-through experience an annual tradition for their kids each Christmas. The mother explained to me that this year, however, their daughter didn't seem to have her same enthusiasm about the display as in years past.

"How did you like it?" the mom asked her daughter after they completed the drive-through, noticing her quiet demeanor.

"It bothered me," she said.

"Really, why was that?" her mom asked.

"Because Jesus hasn't grown at all since last year. He's still a baby!"

That little girl was onto something.

In my many years of talking about Jesus, I am convinced that one of the biggest problems people have with Christianity is that their thoughts about Him have not yet "grown up."

The Problem of a "Half-Remembered Jesus"

A lot of people have a childlike concept of who Jesus is based on Christmas stories or other Bible stories they learned when they were young, but their thoughts about Him have not progressed much from there. In our increasingly post-Christian, secular American culture, many people are somewhat limited in their exposure to the basic tenets of Christianity.

The result is often a strange mixture of cultural religion and Christian tradition that has little resemblance to actual biblical faith. Many people in our culture have a concept of Jesus that has been held in a kind of childlike suspension. This view is lampooned in the comical Ricky Bobby character in the movie *Talladega Nights* who prefers a "little baby Jesus in a ghost manger" and doesn't like to think of a "grown-up Jesus." But that concept of Jesus doesn't work in today's world.

A couple of recent landmark studies points to this problem. Notre Dame sociologist, Christian Smith, conducted a massive research study on the spirituality of young people in America and documented what they actually believe about God. He described their belief system as "moralistic therapeutic deism." In other words, American young people believe in a God who wants His creatures to behave, wants them to feel good about themselves, and is not necessarily involved in their lives on a personal level. [1]

Kenda Creasy Dean, in her book about similar research titled *Almost Christian*, made the observation that many American teenagers who were raised in evangelical churches are not really Christians at all in the traditional, biblical sense of the word. Because they lack basic understanding of the teaching of the Gospel, they are "Christian-ish," but not really Christian. [2]

What has gone wrong? The most obvious conclusion we can draw is that most Christian young people have been exposed to the highlights of Christianity, but have not been taught to see the comprehensive nature of the Bible through the lens of the Gospel. But it is not enough to be "Christian-ish." To accept Jesus is to accept him with all of your heart, strength, and mind.

Well-known Bible scholar, J.B. Phillips, wrote a book titled *Your God Is Too Small*. He proposes that most people who think about Christianity interpret the meaning of Jesus through their own conscience and limited exposure to the biblical narrative, and this self-interpretation leads them to a tragic misunderstanding of His true nature. He insists that if people would take the time to actually think about what the Bible teaches about the bigness and true nature of Jesus, it would change their lives.

He writes:

> *Many people who have a vague childish affection for a half-remembered Jesus have never used their adult critical faculties on the matter at all. They hardly seem to see the paramount importance of His claim to be God. Yet if for one moment we imagine the claim to be true the mind almost reels at its significance.* [3]

Expanding Your Perspective

A good first step in understanding the true nature of Jesus is an expanded perspective on the Christmas story. Most people think the story of Jesus begins with His birth in a manger. Most biographics of famous people begin with their birth, and so it only stands to reason that the story of Jesus would begin this way as well. But the Christmas story is not merely the story of a birth, it is more importantly the account of the miraculous Advent. The real size and scope of the story of Jesus is exponentially bigger than just the manger scene. The word "Advent" comes from the Latin "adventus" and means "arrival." The clear implication is that Christmas is not about a beginning as much as it is about the arrival of the long-awaited Messiah. As we will see, it was an event that was greatly anticipated before its occurrence and was providentially unfolded onto the historical landscape.

Christopher Wright, commenting on the opening of the Gospel of Matthew, says this:

> *Why is it that Matthew will not allow us to join in the adoration of the Magi until we have ploughed through his tedious list of begettings? Why can't we just get on with the story? Because, says Matthew, you won't understand the story—the one I'm about to tell you—unless you see it in light of a much larger story which goes back for many centuries, but leads up to the Jesus you want to know about.* [4]

So to tell the true story of Advent, one has to go back many years before that first Christmas night and look into ages past. It is to take a long look into the unfolding history before Mary and Joseph's fateful journey to Bethlehem. Therefore, at Christmas, we should not think of the birth of the child in the manger as the beginning of Christian history. Instead, we should see it as the culmination of God's eternal plan that was predicted, foreshadowed, and anticipated by centuries of sage prophets, poets, and scribes who lived many hundreds of years before the first Advent. In fact, in the course of this book, we will see that when taken all together, the prophecies, foreshadowing, and typology of the Old Testament that point to the coming of Jesus is one of the most compelling proofs of the validity of the Christian claims. A "grown-up" faith understands the profound implications of this broader view. That is the subject of the next chapter.

Reflect:

Read 1 Corinthians 13:10-12 out loud and think about the implication of these words. Why is it important to think of Jesus in a "grown-up" way? Are there areas in your own spiritual life that are suspended in time? How does knowing and understanding the teaching in the Old Testament of the Messiah help our faith to mature?

Three: What Are the Chances?

But you, Bethlehem Ephrathah,
though you are small among the clans of Judah,
out of you will come for me
one who will be ruler over Israel,
whose origins are from of old,
from ancient times (Micah 5:2).

What makes the story of Jesus so compelling is not only how He came or what He did when He got here (although that is most significant of course), but also how His coming was foreshadowed. If I was wanting to prove to you the validity of the Bible, the many claims of Christianity, and of Jesus Himself, a great place for me to start would be the sheer number of predictions of the coming Messiah that were written about in the centuries before His birth, and how some fifty were fulfilled in minute detail. After all, there have been many who have claimed to be a messiah down through the years, but only one actually had people predict He would come for hundreds of years before His actual birth and then had those prophecies fulfilled. We will address many of these in this book, but first I want us to deal with the implications of the fulfillment of these prophecies.

The Probability of Random Fulfillment

It is one thing to make predictions, it is another thing

altogether to have those predictions actually come true. Think of it like this—the more predictions that are made about the future coming Messiah, and the more detail given in those predictions make the likelihood of their random fulfillment exponentially less likely. What are the chances that one could predict the exact place of birth for some future leader 500 years before his birth? That is exactly what Micah did in the passage above. Further, what are the chances that hundreds of years before some future leader, one could predict the following:

> How He would be born (Isaiah 7:14)
> From what tribe he would come? (Genesis 49:10)
> That He would flee to Egypt (Hosea 11:1)
> The circumstances surrounding His birth (Jeremiah 31:15)
> A messenger would prepare the way (Isaiah 40:3-5)
> He would be rejected (Psalm 69:8)
> That He would be betrayed (Psalm 41:9)
> The circumstances of His death (Psalm 22)

The fact that even one of the above predictions would come true is a mathematical improbability. But the fact that all of them came true is a seemingly mathematical impossibility.

The mathematical probability of eight fulfilled prophecies has actually been calculated. Dr. Peter Stoner, former Professor at Westmont College in Santa Monica, California, did an extensive analysis and determined that the probability of predicting the birth place of Jesus, based on the population of the earth at the time, is one in 300,000. But the chances of eight prophecies being fulfilled altogether is one in ten with seventeen zeroes!

To understand what that probability looks like, Dr. Stoner gives this illustration:

> *If you mark one of ten tickets, place all the tickets in a hat, thoroughly stir them, and then ask a blindfolded man to draw one, his chance of getting the right ticket is one in ten. Suppose that we take 10^17 silver dollars and lay them on the face of Texas. They'll cover all of the state two feet deep. Now mark one of these silver dollars and stir the whole mass thoroughly, all over the state. Blindfold a man and tell him that he can travel as far as he wishes, but he must pick up one silver dollar and say that this is the right one.* [5]

What Does It Prove?

Of course there are many more than just eight prophecies, and so it is easy to see that the culmination of all of them being fulfilled is powerful evidence indeed. But what does it prove? Let's consider three important conclusions:

First of all, it proves that there was intentionality and providence in the coming of Jesus.

Back during the cold war, a man named David Greenglass sold nuclear secrets to the Soviet Union. His conspirators planned a meeting at their embassy in Mexico City and arranged for him to identify himself utilizing a series of six consecutive signs. They were as follows:

1. Sign his name as I. Jackson to the secretary at the embassy.
2. After three days, go to Plaza de Colon.
3. Stand before the statue of Columbus.
4. Put his middle finger in a guide book.
5. When he was approached, he was to say it was a nice statue.
6. Say he was from Oklahoma. [6]

As you can imagine, when the Soviet conspirators observed all six of these signs, they were convinced he was Greenglass. Why? Because the probability of all of these things happening in sequence was statistically impossible unless it was indeed Greenglass coming there according to the pre-planned arrangement. In a similar way, when one truly understands and observes the signs of the coming of Jesus that were foretold in the Old Testament Scriptures, there is no denying that the arrangements leading to His coming were pre-arranged. There was definite intentionality and providence in His coming.

Secondly, it proves that Jesus is God. Only the divine

Creator of the universe would have the kind of power that could dictate the time, place, and events surrounding His own coming.

Years ago, I was discussing the doctrine of the incarnation with a Muslim student in Amman, Jordan. He explained to me that the idea that God could become man was an offensive one to the Muslim. "Do you believe that God could do anything he wanted to do?" I asked him.

"Of course!" was his answer.

"So do Christians," I told him, "and because we have such a high view of the power and ability of God, we believe that He could be born of a virgin, live among men, die on a cross, and resurrect three days later if he wanted!"

Thirdly and most importantly, it proves that God is a good and loving God. Only a God who was good and loving would have such compassion for His creation that despite our rebelliousness and sin, would choose to redeem us at such great personal cost. In the 4th century A.D., Athanasius wrote this in his book *On the Incarnation*:

> *Such indifference to the ruin of His own work before His very eyes would argue not goodness in God but limitation and that far more than if He had never created men at all. It is impossible, therefore, that God should leave man to be carried off by corruption, because it would be unfitting and unworthy of Himself.* [7]

The Bible says that God's love for us is revealed by the fact that He was willing to come to the earth and die for us. But even more than that, He knew our sin before-hand, that "while we were yet sinners," He was willing to come and die for us in spite of that knowledge. So as you can see, it is not just an interesting curiosity that so many prophecies point us to the coming of Jesus. The fact that Jesus came to us in this way proves some very important truths about what we believe about God and His work in our lives. It is not only important that we understand these things as proof about the nature of God and the validity of Scripture, but also as we will see in the next chapter, it is important in how we read and understand the Bible.

Reflect:

Read Micah 5:2. Why is it important that Jesus was predicted hundreds of years before His birth? How does the fact that Jesus' coming being anticipated throughout the Old Testament give proof to the validity of the Bible and of Christianity? What does it mean to you personally that God cared enough about His creation to come to Earth in this way? How does this teaching affect what we believe about God's love? In what ways do these things strengthen your faith?

Four: What is the Meaning of this Bible?

> *Concerning this salvation, the prophets, who spoke of the grace that was to come to you, searched intently and with the greatest care, trying to find out the time and circumstances to which the Spirit of Christ in them was pointing when he predicted the sufferings of the Messiah and the glories that would follow. It was revealed to them that they were not serving themselves but you, when they spoke of the things that have now been told you by those who have preached the gospel to you by the Holy Spirit sent from heaven. Even angels long to look into these things (1 Peter 1:10-12).*

Let's suppose you meet someone who is interested in learning about the Bible. Let's say this person has absolutely no prior knowledge about Christianity, or about what it contains, or even who wrote it. But out of deep curiosity because of all the people in the world who say they believe it, this person would like for you to explain its meaning over a series of meetings. "Could you take the time over the next few weeks to explain it to me?" this person asks. You enthusiastically set up a meeting with your new friend, and the two of you decide to meet once a week over a cup of coffee for an hour or two at a time.

Where would you start? It would be very difficult to start in the conventional way by just opening up the massive collection of sixty-six books, pointing to the table of contents, and explaining the authors and content of each of the volumes. Do you begin by giving a history of the Jewish religion? What would you say was the Bible's main thesis? In what ways could you begin a series of conversations like this without overwhelming this person with history, theology, or even your own particular bias?

I think the answer lies in an interesting story that is found at the end of the Gospel of Luke after the resurrection of Jesus. This story is unique in that it gives us an insight into how Jesus Himself might answer this question.

The story begins with two men who were disciples of Jesus traveling down the road to Emmaus after the crucifixion. While they were walking along discussing the horrible events they had just witnessed, the resurrected Christ suddenly appeared with them and walked beside them. These men were very upset about the crucifixion of their leader but did not realize that He was there right next to them.

They knew that all of Jerusalem had turned against their band of Jesus followers, and they were retreating from this intense situation in Jerusalem. They were on the run and devastated by the day's events. Jesus asked them to explain why they were in such a dark mood. They were surprised that He was the last to know, but politely began to explain to this stranger what had happened. That is when Jesus gives them this answer:

> *He said to them, "How foolish you are, and how slow to believe all that the prophets have spoken! Did not the*

Messiah have to suffer these things and then enter his glory?" And beginning with Moses and all the Prophets, he explained to them what was said in all the Scriptures concerning himself (Luke 24:25-27).

So here is the answer to the question of how one begins to explain the Bible to a new friend. What we have in this passage is a perfect example of the problem many people have in understanding the meaning of the Bible. Most people come to the Bible looking for answers to life's most complex and distressing issues and have no idea how to approach it. My experience has been that most people only come to the Bible when they feel they really need it. And usually that is after some personal crisis. In a similar way, these men are reeling from a tragic event that has rocked their world. They are grieving from the loss of a spiritual leader on whom they had staked their lives. They no doubt grieved not only for the loss of life, but also for the loss of a dream and perhaps even the loss of hope itself. They are afraid and anxious, maybe even depressed. They are looking for answers. It is not hard to imagine that they are talking to one another about life's deepest and most important question—what is life's meaning?

It is in that moment that Jesus appears to them. And yet they have no idea who is standing with them. For some reason, Jesus in His resurrected state is unrecognizable to these men who had followed Him as their teacher. It isn't until Jesus opens up the Old Testament to them, and beginning with the law and the prophets, exposes the true meaning of the text that they can see that all of Scripture is about Him. After this explanation, they suddenly recognize who Jesus is, and their hearts are changed.

What a great picture of what happens to us when we have the true meaning of the Scriptures opened to us!

So if I am helping someone who has no prior knowledge of the Bible to understand its meaning, I would start with this story. I would say, "Jesus is the interpretive key to understanding all of the Bible—including the Old Testament."

You Should Have Seen Me Coming

Another story similar to this one is found in John 5. In this passage, Jesus scolds some Old Testament teachers and scholars for not recognizing him:

> *You study the Scriptures diligently because you think that in them you have eternal life. These are the very Scriptures that testify about me, yet you refuse to come to me to have life (John 5:39-40).*

Jesus tells them that all of Old Testament Scripture bears witness to His identity. This can only mean that God is the one who orchestrated all of the events and history of the Old Testament as a way to point people to the coming Messiah. The Old Testament Scriptures point to the ultimate solution and answer culminating in the work of Christ. He says this in verse 56:

If you believed Moses, you would believe me, for he wrote about me.

Remarkably, Jesus is saying that all of the writings of Moses, in addition to the writings of the prophets, are all pointing to *Him*. In other words, Jesus is saying to these religious leaders who have spent their lives pouring over the mosaic law and narrative of the Torah:

If you had read it carefully, you would have seen me coming!

This can only mean that if a person reads the Old Testament in the way God intends, they would find the parallels to Jesus' coming obvious. It means that carefully reading it this way leads a person to anticipate it, long for it, and expect it. Jesus' message to the students of the Scriptures is that if they had read it this way, then when Jesus did appear, it would have been obvious to them who He was.

One of my favorite examples of this is found at the beginning of Luke's Gospel. Dr. Luke tells the story of a very devout man who studied the Old Testament promises faithfully and believed he would live to see the Messiah. The account of what happens through the work of the Holy Spirit when he sees the baby Jesus is especially poignant:

Now there was a man in Jerusalem called Simeon, who was righteous and devout. He was waiting for the consolation of Israel, and the Holy Spirit was on him. It had been revealed to him by the Holy Spirit that he would not die before he had seen the Lord's Messiah. Moved by the Spirit, he went into the temple courts. When the parents brought in the child Jesus to do for him what the custom of the Law required, Simeon took him in his arms and praised God, saying:

Sovereign Lord, as you have promised,
you may now dismiss your servant in peace.
For my eyes have seen your salvation,
which you have prepared in the sight of all nations:
a light for revelation to the Gentiles,
and the glory of your people Israel (Luke 2:25-32).

This is an important pattern for us to remember. It is a combination of the careful reading of Scripture and sensitivity to the Holy Spirit working in us that brings clarity to our understanding of Jesus.

Old Testament scholar Graeme Goldsworthy wrote this:

We do not start at Genesis 1 and work our way forward until we discover where it is all leading. Rather we first come to Christ, and He directs us to study the Old Testament in the light of the gospel. The gospel will interpret the Old Testament by showing us its goal and meaning. [8]

This is a remarkable truth that most people who read the Bible for the first time don't understand. Reading through the Old Testament can be frustrating and confusing if you don't understand this one important truth. The key to understanding the Bible is to read it through the lens of the Gospel. We first come to Christ, and then He directs our study, which is to say to read it through the lens of all that Jesus is and all that Jesus does. Once we have determined to look at the Scripture in this way, it opens up to us in new and exciting ways. Stories, events, laws, and teachings that once made no sense and seemed to have no bearing on our lives suddenly come to life and have new relevance.

So now that we have established how we will begin to help our new friend see the purpose and meaning of the Bible, we are ready to sit down with our first cup of coffee and think about the implications of this simple truth.

Reflect:

Read 1 Peter 1:10-12. This passage clearly reveals that the Old Testament points us to the coming of Jesus. Why is it important to embrace the Old Testament Scriptures as we study and learn about our faith? How does ignoring the Old Testament hurt our ability to understand the narrative of Scripture?

Five: Power in His Name

Therefore God exalted him to the highest place
and gave him the name that is above every name,
that at the name of Jesus every knee should bow,
in heaven and on earth and under the earth,
and every tongue acknowledge that Jesus Christ is Lord,
to the glory of God the Father (Philippians 2:9-11).

Have you noticed how fascinated people are with Jesus? The question, "What do you think of Jesus?" almost always elicits a lively discussion. Even people who are ambiguous or spiteful toward religion, in general, seem to always have a strong opinion about the carpenter from Galilee. You only have to say the name "Jesus" in a crowded place, and people notice. If you simply say the name in public, people's ears seem to perk up, and heads turn. How interesting that people never seem to use the names of Buddha, Krishna, Moses, or Mohammad as profanity but will use the name of Jesus. Why is that? I believe it is because there is provocative power in that name, even for the most ardent unbeliever.

I once had a discussion with a graduate student who was particularly put out with evangelical Christianity. In his opinion, the American church was nothing more than a grand ponzi scheme that made empty promises and taught fairy tales. It is often hard to know when to start a conversation about Christianity when people seem to be so cynical.

But when I asked him what he thought of Jesus, his demeanor changed. He told me that he believed the teachings of Jesus were significantly important. He liked Jesus' emphasis on loving your neighbor, forgiving others, and taking care of the poor. "I like Jesus," he said, "I just don't like religion!"

I explained to him that although I disagreed with his thinking about the church, I could completely agree with him about religion. I know it sounds odd for a pastor to say this, but I don't like religion either! In fact, I see religion as being a major problem in our world. I believe religion inoculates people from a true understanding of Jesus.

I told him I had staked my life on the life, teaching, and work of Jesus, but *not* religion. I told him I believe religion is man's attempt to build a bridge to ultimate reality (or God), and yet Christianity is based upon the belief that God Himself has built a bridge to man in the person and work of Jesus Christ. Religion is about our works. Christianity is about Christ's work. Religion is about doing good things *so that* you will be accepted, while Christianity is about doing good things *because* you've been accepted and brought in. There is a big difference between the two.

The purpose of this book, in fact, is to help people clear up all of the fog that surrounds a true understanding of Jesus, the meaning of the Bible, and find the kind of clarity those disciples on the road to Emmaus experienced after Jesus opened up the Scriptures to them.

What is Most Important

Jesus is without a doubt the most intriguing, controversial, misquoted, and misunderstood figure in human history. But the audacity of the claims of Jesus in the New Testament cannot be ignored. And the thoroughness of the foreshadowing of Jesus in the Old Testament leading up to His coming cannot be denied. The Scriptures from Genesis to Revelation help us to find the true Jesus. And to find Jesus is to find life. This is why the Apostle Paul wrote this remarkable statement in 1 Corinthians 2:2:

> *I was resolved to know nothing while I was with you except Jesus Christ and Him crucified.*

He is saying there is absolutely nothing more important to know or understand than to know and understand Jesus, and what He did for us. This is the content of the entire Bible. It is, in a sense, resolved to help us know nothing except Jesus Christ and Him crucified. Once a person realizes that this is the key to understanding all of the Bible, even obscure Old Testament passages that never made sense before begin to become clear in light of that truth.

But Paul is also saying something very important about how we use our time. When he says, "I was resolved to know nothing while I was with you," he was saying that the time we have with each other is finite and therefore needs to be used purposefully. He wasn't going to waste his time with his Corinthian friends with mere small talk. He was resolved to use his time to deal with ultimate things. So here is the lesson—if I only have a short time with the people God has placed in my life, I want to use that time to help people know and understand the real Jesus, and what He came to this earth to accomplish.

So this is what my time is for and what the Bible contains. Each of us should say something like this to ourselves:

> *I have a short time on Earth with the people God has put in my life, and therefore, I should use it to point them to what is most important—the life and work of Jesus!*

In the following pages, we explore together how the Old Testament does just that. We will see that the most controversial and often misunderstood person in history, whose name carries more power than any other name, is the key to understanding the meaning of the law, the prophets, and poets in the Hebrew script.

My hope is that this book will help equip you to have deeper and more meaningful conversations with others not only about the interpretation, but also about the intentionality of Old Testament Scripture. I believe if you approach your study in this way, God will open all kinds of exciting opportunities for you to share what you know!

Both Testaments Point to Jesus

For many years of my Christian life, I thought of the Old

Testament as nothing more than a kind of warm-up act for the New Testament. Like most Christians I have known, I found the first testament to be difficult to understand and even more difficult to explain. I tended to focus most of my study and attention on the New Testament. After all, Jesus had come and fulfilled the law, and in my mind that meant He had displaced the law. Though the Old Testament was good to know in that it foreshadowed Christ, it was really the New Testament that deserved my time and attention. I was eager to learn how to share the Gospel and all of the training tools I found focused exclusively on New Testament passages.

After years of teaching the Bible and pastoring, it took a trip to the Middle East to open my eyes to the power of the Old Testament to point people to Jesus.

It happened on a hiking trip in southern Jordan near Petra. Some friends and I were invited to have dinner with a Bedouin tribal leader and several members of his clan. The leader of our group was a young archaeologist who was a devoted follower of Jesus. Before meeting the members of this tribe, we prayed that God would give us an opportunity to talk about the Gospel. We only had one meeting with them, and we would try to use it to talk about what was most important to us.

I remember walking into the tent to meet our new friends and thinking, "We have almost nothing in common with these men. They live in an isolated desert in the Middle East, they speak only Arabic and read only the Quran, and have never before met Americans."

As it turned out, the one thing we did have in common was an appreciation for the Torah, the parts of the Old Testament attributed to Moses. It was knowledge of the Old Testament and how it leads us to Jesus that gave us an amazing opportunity in the few hours we spent with them.

Our time together began with small talk about archeology. The tribal leader was fascinated with that work and anxious to tell us about an experience he had as a boy working on an archaeological dig. He told us that one morning he and a friend jumped into a pit on the dig site and landed right next to a snake. At this point, my archaeologist friend translated what the tribal leader had just said and told me, "Everyone around here has a snake story!"

When he finished telling his story, the circle applauded in appreciation. There was an awkward silence for a few seconds, and then my friend spoke up and said, "There is a story in the Bible about the Israelites getting bitten by snakes. Would you like to hear it?"

"Yes, please," was their answer.

Nodding at me, he said to them, "My friend here is a Bible teacher in America and knows this story well. I'd like for him to tell it."

In the next several minutes, I recounted the story from Numbers 21 of how the Israelites had rebelled against

God, and the result was that they were inflicted with the bites of poisonous snakes. When Moses cried out to God on their behalf, God's solution was for Moses to lift up a bronze snake so that anyone who looked upon that snake was healed of the poison. I could see from everyone's reaction that the story had resonated with them. There was great appreciation in this culture of good stories—especially stories from the Bible. Sociologists tell us that much of the developing world is an "oral culture" as opposed to the written culture of the West. This means that most of their education and learning comes through the use of stories.

I went on to explain that Christians have been given the explanation of why this story was so important. I explained that it was a foreshadowing of something that would occur hundreds of years later. In John 3, Jesus told an expert in the Old Testament Scriptures, a man by the name of Nicodemus, that "just as the snake was lifted up in the wilderness, so the Son of Man must be lifted up."

I told them that Jesus Himself had given the explanation of the meaning of this strange story. I told them that each of us has sinned, and the result was a kind of poison of the human heart. Just as the Israelites had rebelled against God, and their rebellion had resulted in a deadly poison, in almost the exact same way all of our hearts have been poisoned by our sinful rebellion.

I explained that this poison was so devastating that we are all moving toward eternal death and destruction. Our only hope is found in the fact that Jesus Christ had offered Himself as payment for our sin and had been "lifted up" on the cross as a way of satisfying the justice and righteousness of God. And that just as the Israelites looked to the bronze snake, anyone who looks to Jesus will be healed of their poison.

The tribal leader looked at me thoughtfully and then said finally, "This is a very interesting story!"

I knew in that moment that God had miraculously allowed a connection to be made, although we were separated from these men both by language and culture, and that our way of life and worldview were separated as far as the thousands of miles between Oklahoma City and Showbak, Jordan. In those few minutes sitting together in that tent, the Old Testament had opened the way to the Gospel with our new friends.

That experience changed everything for me.

It ignited a new reality that continues to this day. Could it be that the Old Testament had been hard to understand not because it was overshadowed by the promises of the New Testament, but because I had been reading it in the wrong way? I had been guilty of the same problem many generations of Christians had experienced in their understanding of the Old Testament.

An extreme example of this misunderstanding is the heresy of "marcionism." Marcion of Sinope was a second-century priest who came to believe that Jesus was the Savior sent by God and Paul, His chief apostle, but that the Hebrew Bible was to be rejected because it described an angry, vengeful God of Israel who was separate from the all-forgiving God of the New Testament. His followers were known as "marcionites," and they carried around a Bible that left out any reference to the Old Testament.

When I looked into my own heart and spiritual journey, I could see that by ignoring the significance of the Old Testament, I had been guilty of a lesser version of marcionism. Though I never would have admitted it, I subconsciously pushed aside any interest in the Old Testament because I saw it as irrelevant when compared to the New Testament. I fear this is a malady that has affected many Christians!

But I now read the Old Testament Scriptures in a completely different way. I no longer view it as merely foreshadowing the work of the New Testament. Instead, I read every page and every book with the understanding that in the whole, it is pointing us to Jesus and the Gospel. In the coming pages, I will attempt to show you how this process works.

Reflect:

Read Philippians 2:9-11. Say the name of Jesus out loud. What do you think about as you say that name? Why do you believe the name of Jesus has such power? Why is it so important to see the Bible as primarily about Jesus? Do you believe most people see the Bible in this way? Why or why not? How do you think your own opinion of the Old Testament can be changed by reading it through the lens of the Gospel?

PART TWO
Story

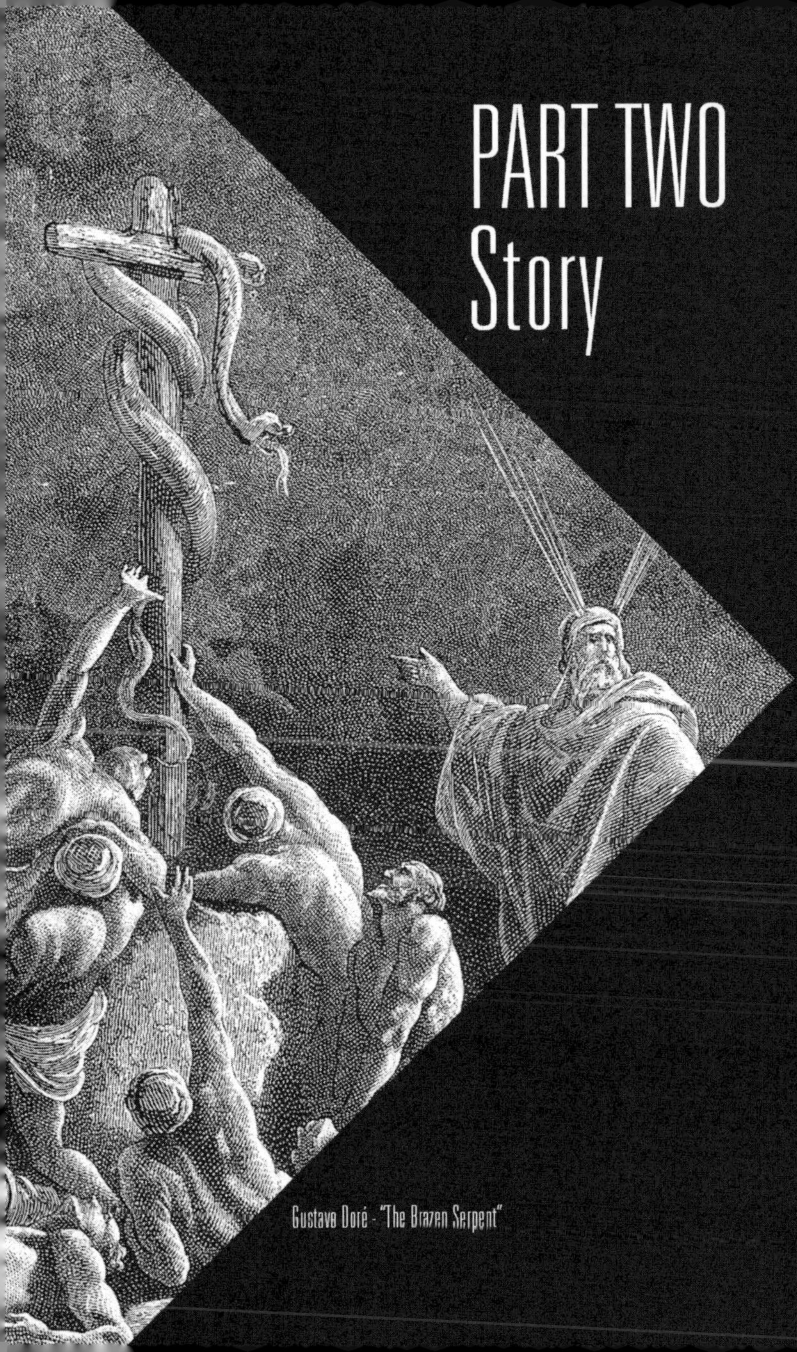

Gustave Doré - "The Brazen Serpent"

Six: The Power of a Good Story

These were all commended for their faith, yet none of them received what had been promised since God had planned something better for us so that only together with us would they be made perfect (Hebrews 11:39-40).

One thing I have learned through the years, as one who makes a living as a public speaker, is the power of a good story. In my teaching, I could go on and on about this textual nuance or that historical fact, but if I go too long in that direction, people's eyes start drifting away from my eyes, and attention spans begin to wane. Believe me, I've heard all the jokes about preachers putting people to sleep! My dad, who was also a pastor, used to say, "One time I had a dream that I was preaching, and then I woke up and realized I actually was preaching!"

People get worn out by too many words.

But the minute I start telling a story, people's heads start snapping back up, and eyes start locking back in. There is great power in a story. I believe that this is the reason the Bible is filled with one compelling story after another. God gave us stories to help us understand what is most important in life. He gave us stories to keep our attention. This is why it is so vitally important to study the underlying meaning of all of these stories.

The Bible is Not a Morality Play

We also have to be careful with the stories. It is tempting to view the Bible and especially the Old Testament as a giant morality play. As parents and teachers, we are tempted to look to various stories within Scripture and point out a particular moral to teach our children. We look to Joseph as an example of how to resist temptation, to David for courage to face giants, and to Joshua for leadership in crossing the Jordan and so on. Although there is certain value in helping children learn valuable lessons from biblical texts, it is a big mistake to read the Bible as one would read Aesop's fables. Aesop's famous stories were written as a way to point children to particular values. The stories themselves were fantasy, but the value in them was to bring about a strong, moral lesson. In a similar way, some people see the Old Testament stories as nothing more than a good way to teach moral lessons. The primary problem with this approach to reading the Old Testament is that it ignores the bigger issue each of these stories addresses and can point instead to a kind of man centered, religious moralism.

The biblical stories are not fantasy, but rather a historical account of God's providential purpose. Unless one sees that the entire Bible is the story of how God has fulfilled His redemptive plan and how that story will conclude in a final culmination of His work at the end of history, then many of the stories taken individually would actually send a conflicting moral message. Because after all, there is really only one true hero in the Bible, and that is God Himself.

One of the most compelling things about the Bible is how honest it is about the main characters. Adam was a passive husband, Cain was a murderer, Noah was a drunk, Abraham, Isaac and Jacob were considered the fathers of Israel, and yet each of them had serious moral failures. Jacob was a deceiver, Moses had anger issues, David was an adulterer, Eli was a workaholic and a terrible father. Jonah was a rebellious prophet who was angry with God while reluctantly carrying out God's commands. Reading the patriarchs and the prophets is a sordid tale of strange behavior and blatant disobedience, even as God was using them to bring about His message of redemption.

It is as if the authors of the Bible go out of their way to show what sinful slouches men are, and how gloriously forgiving and gracious is God. If there is a moral to each of these stories, it is that man is a complete failure when it comes to obeying God. Though we can learn certain moral lessons from each of these stories, they all point us to a larger story. The stories tell us something significant about ourselves and about God, but it is not your typical Aesop morality ethic. Because in every story, man is the problem. The only solution is found in God's redemptive plan.

God's Love Story

So instead of reading the Bible as a giant morality play, it is better to think of it as the story of God's love. Each of the stories within the Bible points to the one overriding theme of His plan to redeem His creation by great love. That is its meta-narrative. When we know the meta-narrative, or the underlying reason for the stories, they come alive in a much deeper and more powerful way. The great 19th-century English pastor, Charles Spurgeon, says this:

> *I have never yet found a text that had not got a road to Christ in it, and if I ever do find one that has not a road to Christ in it, I will make one; I will go over hedge and ditch but I would get at my Master, for the sermon cannot do any good unless there is a savor of Christ in it.*[9]

As one reads the stories of the Old Testament, one should always keep in mind that God has a bigger story to tell, and we are part of that story. How our story intersects with His is of ultimate importance to each of us. In the following pages, my hope is to show how none of the wonderful stories in the Old Testament can be fully understood unless seen within the context of the greatest story of all.

Reflect:

Read Hebrews 11:39-40. What does it mean to you that "you and I are a part of God's story"? In what ways have you seen God work in your life? In your family's life? Why is it significant that God had "planned something different" even in the midst of the stories of the Old Testament believers? What does this mean for your story? Why is it important to not think of the Bible as a morality play? What is the true moral of the story of the Bible?

Seven: Setting the Stage

In the beginning God created the heavens and the earth (Genesis 1:1).

In the beginning was the Word, and the Word was with God, and the Word was God. He was with God in the beginning. Through him all things were made; without him nothing was made that has been made. In him was life, and that life was the light of all mankind. The light shines in the darkness, and the darkness has not overcome it (John 1:1-5).

By faith we understand that the universe was formed at God's command, so that what is seen was not made out of what was visible (Hebrews 11:3).

For in him all things were created: things in heaven and on earth, visible and invisible, whether thrones or powers or rulers or authorities; all things have been created through him and for him. He is before all things, and in him all things hold together (Colossians 1:16-17).

What if I told you that the stage was set for the work of Christ not in Bethlehem, but at the creation event? This is the reason that John begins his Gospel not with the story of the manger, but with the words, "In the beginning." How is that true? After all, Jesus was a humble, Jewish carpenter born in Bethlehem in Judea and raised in Nazareth somewhere around 1 A.D. (The actual date was probably closer to 6 B.C.)

All of this is stated in the biblical text. But as we have already established in previous chapters, to truly understand the nature of Jesus Christ of Nazareth is to understand that His birth was pre-conceived and foreshadowed in the Old Testament Scriptures. But before I can explain how all of those Scriptures lead to Christ, I need to point out that the creation event itself ushers in His pre-ordained, redemptive work.

To understand the first few chapters of Genesis is to understand the context in which it was written. My New Testament professor in seminary was Dr. Thomas Lea. Dr. Lea used to say to his class of young pastors, "Always remember when you are teaching that the Bible never says what the Bible never said." By that, he meant that it is essential when studying any text of Scripture to know its original context. So when we ask what is the original context of the first two chapters of the book of Genesis, the answer is best articulated by Dr. Richard Pratt, who pointed out that Moses wrote the first few chapters to the nation of Israel as a way of helping them to see God's work in redemptive history. He writes that it was written "to teach the Israelites God's design for them as a nation through the background of early world history and the lives of their patriarchs."[10]

These chapters, inspired by God and ultimately written to each of us, were not just an account of the creation event.

They were originally written to Israel, a redeemed people in a fallen world. They were written to help them see that they were to look to a greater redeemer than Moses, who had a greater redemption than mere physical liberation from Egyptian slavery in store. He was teaching them that God created the heavens and the earth for a specific purpose, and that before even one star was put into place, God knew of His redemptive plan. All of creation was made for this purpose! David Murray wrote this:

> *There was a redemptive plan before there was a creation. Jesus the Redeemer was the Lamb slain from the foundation of the world (Revelation 13:8); indeed, His saving work was foreordained BEFORE the creation of the world. The Father, Son and Holy Spirit arranged to redeem the world before they created the world. They created the world with a view of redeeming it.* [11]

When we read the first chapter of Genesis, we need to remember that even before any of the events described took place, there was already a plan in place for the redemption of the world. God had a plan to redeem us even before He spoke the world into existence. So God created everything in nature, including man himself, with a view of His redemptive work to come.

Understand the Purpose of Creation

Why is it so important to view the Genesis account as primarily an example of how God created the world with redemptive purposes in mind? Because when we view the story in this way, we get beyond the minutia of how the world was created and get to the real issue of why it was created. When I know the purpose of something, it becomes more useful. When I know the purpose of the world's existence, I know my place in it. Too many people go through their entire lives only thinking about their problems from the limited perspective of felt needs or physical constraints. They never step back from their "here and now" wants and needs to think about ultimate questions like, "How did I get here?" or "Why am I here?"

Dr. David Martin Lloyd Jones makes this point in his book, *The Gospel in Genesis*. He says that one can only truly understand the meaning of life by looking at it from the larger context of eternity. He writes the following:

> *We are right in the midst of it, and we cannot see it for we are too near it. There are times when to see a thing you must get away from it. If you want to know England truly, travel abroad.* [12]

This has certainly been true in my own experience. I didn't fully understand the nuances of my own country until I started traveling to other countries. It was from a distance that I gained a greater appreciation of my own culture and identity. Lloyd Jones, who was both a medical doctor and a pastor, made the further point that a medical diagnosis should never be limited to simply observing a patient's symptoms.

In a similar way, if you see your life from a perspective that is broad enough, you can begin to get to the real issues that can lead to ultimate solutions. Paul the Apostle leads us to the big idea that if we look at all of life on its grand scale of eternity and creation, we can get to life's ultimate purpose:

> *For since the creation of the world, God's invisible qualities—his eternal power and divine nature—have been clearly seen, being understood from what has been made, so that people are without excuse (Romans 1:20).*

So if God created the world with His redemptive plan in mind, it can only mean that all of the events of creation and even creation itself reveal the intricacies of that plan. The famous 18th-century New England theologian, Jonathan Edwards, wrote that this world "was doubtless created to be a stage upon which this great and wonderful work of redemption should be transacted."[13] When God created the world, He stepped back from that grand palette and began to create with His design of redemption in mind.

If we see the creation story in this way, the purposefulness of all of creation begins to come into clearer focus. There are countless examples of this laced throughout the creation account, but let me focus on what I think are the five most important:

First of all, we see in the creation story a pattern of redemption that is important.

Notice that there are specific steps in which God created. After all, he could have just created it all at once, but he chose a particular pattern. I believe that pattern points us to something important when we compare those steps to the process of salvation. David Murray summarizes those steps this way:

> Creation and salvation both begin with life-giving Spirit.

> Both created life and salvation life begin with light.

> Both created light and salvation light separate from darkness.

> Both creation and salvation produce fruit.

> Creation and salvation both move toward man's creation in God's image.

> Creation and salvation both culminate in control and dominion. [14]

Second, by creating man with the freedom to choose from the tree of good and evil, God demonstrated man's need for a redemptive solution.

He created man in his own image, and that image was defiled by the sin nature. He created the first Adam who would be the contrast to the second Adam, Jesus. The result was that the first Adam rebelled against the purposes of God, and desiring to be like God, bowed to the temptation of the enemy and grasped the forbidden fruit. But Jesus, who was the perfect image and likeness of God, described by Paul as the "second

Adam," did not consider equality with God as "something to be grasped" (notice the terminology) but was obedient even to death on the cross. Paul says this in Romans 5:17:

> *For if, by the trespass of the one man, death reigned through that one man, how much more will those who receive God's abundant provision of grace and of the gift of righteousness reign in life through the one man, Jesus Christ!*

Third, the creativeness of the world itself leads us to Jesus.

We all understand the concepts of light and darkness because those things are in our consciousness precisely because God created them. And He created them not only for the purposes of nature, but also for the purposes of salvation! When the Bible talks about Jesus as the "light of the world," we know exactly what that means. We know what a blessing an abundant rain provides after a time of drought, but have you considered that maybe God created that process as a way to help us understand His provision in salvation? We are accustomed to thinking of these things in reverse. The fact that God had redemption in mind at creation means that God uses these things that naturally occur as a way to illustrate spiritual truths. The very creation of them was for the purpose of leading us to salvation.

When you see that God created everything for His redemptive purposes, it's easier to think of all aspects of creation in a way that points to that purpose. What about thirst? Or hunger? These are just natural bodily processes, you say. But are they really, or are they instead God's way of helping us to understand how much we need Him? What about the feelings of joy or love? It was through contemplating these emotions that resulted in C.S. Lewis giving up his atheism to follow Christ. It's easy to see that God created these emotions as a way to point us to Him. He created sleep and rest as a way of showing us that He is our rest. God created the very universe and the laws of physics, astronomy, and mathematics as a way to lead us to Him. Nobel Laureate Arno Penzias, co-discoverer of the radiation afterglow, made this amazing admission:

> *Astronomy leads us to a unique event, a universe which was created out of nothing and delicately balanced to provide exactly the conditions required to support life. In the absence of an absurdly-improbable accident, the observations of modern science seem to suggest an underlying, one might say, supernatural plan.* [15]

Think of the many ways God has used His creation to point us to His redemptive plan for salvation in numerous biblical texts. He created birds to teach us not to be anxious. He created sheep to show us how to follow Him. He created lilies and roses to show us how He provides for us. He created seed, soil, and vines to show us how to grow. He created salt and light to show how we should be attracted to Him. He created bread to show us that He is all we need. He created the tree to illustrate life and eventually to bring about the death of His Son.

Fourth, God established certain foreshadowing types in the midst of the creation event that would show us His future redemptive works.

Think of what happened at creation. Out of chaos and darkness, God brought about order, light, and life. In a similar way, our sin causes chaos, darkness, and death. By the work of new life in Christ, He brings order, light, and life into our lives. In Christ, we are a new creation. Old things pass away, and the new has come (2 Corinthians 5:17).

At the creation event, God established the institution of Sabbath Rest to later illustrate how our sinful condition causes restlessness and toil, and when Christ comes into our lives, He brings us into His rest (Matthew 11:28, Hebrews 4:9).

Also, the marriage between Adam and Eve, performed by God Himself in the garden, would come to illustrate the marriage of Christ and His church at the culmination of human history (Revelation 19:6-9, Ephesians 5:21ff). All of these are examples of various types used in the creation event that foreshadow the later redeeming work of Christ.

Finally, the curse that was brought about by man's rebellion gives us a comprehensive understanding of the consequences of our sinful condition.

The biblical account of the fall gives us a vivid picture of what our sin causes. Our sin has brought about death and eternal separation from God. But our separation from God is not the only consequence. The fall caused relational problems between Adam and Eve ("It was the woman you gave me.") It caused physical problems (death and toil). It also caused emotional problems (shame and fear). From the Genesis account of the creation and subsequent fall, we can see that all of our problems can be traced back to the sinful nature we inherited from our father, Adam, and our mother, Eve.

In addition, the murder of Abel by his brother, Cain, was a direct result of the fall. God told Cain that his brother's blood cried out from the ground for justice. The writer of Hebrews would later say that the blood of Jesus "speaks a better word" than the blood of Abel (Hebrews 12:24). The blood of Abel represents the cry for justice in our fallen world. The blood of Jesus speaks a better word because it cries out for mercy and grace.

So as you can see, the story of Christ certainly does not just begin at a crowded Bethlehem inn on a silent night in a manger of straw. It was well established in the eternal void before creation. In fact, His redemptive work was woven within the very fabric of God's creative design. Truly, the story of creation is where we all must begin in order to understand our need for salvation. But this story is only the beginning. As we read through the Old Testament, stories within *the* story begin to come alive as we look at them from the perspective of His eternal purposes. That is the subject of the next few chapters.

Reflect:

Read Colossians 1:16-17. What does it mean to you that God created everything with Jesus' redemptive plan in mind? How does knowing this about creation change the way you think about nature? How about the way you think of God's design? Can you think of examples in your own life of the beauty of God's creation pointing you to His love? Do you believe the beauty of creation is a strong argument for a creator? Why or why not? Does it seem logical to you that the creation story points us to Jesus? Why or why not?

Eight: From Noah to Babylon

For as were the days of Noah, so will be the coming of the Son of Man (Matthew 24:37).

Before we go any further in our exploration of the Old Testament to see how it points us to the coming of Jesus, I need to stop and describe the use of typology in Scripture.

The Meaning of Old Testament Typology

Typology is a literary device that is very important in understanding the way the Old Testament points to Jesus. In essence, a typology is a picture that is painted for us in the Old Testament in order to lead us to a future spiritual truth in the New Testament. In this sense, it foreshadows a future person, place, or event.

One of the most interesting things about Old Testament types is that it demonstrates the eternal nature of God's unfolding history. In this way, He uses people and events from one point in time in order to foreshadow a greater truth at another point in time. A type or anti-type is a person or event in the historical record that God uses to point to another literal historical person or event at another time in history.

When we talk about types in this way, we are not talking about allegories, which are fictional stories representing a truth that are not actual historical events. The concept of biblical typology actually comes from the New Testament itself. One classic example is from the Apostle Paul in 1 Corinthians 10:1-6:

> *For I do not want you to be ignorant of the fact, brothers and sisters, that our ancestors were all under the cloud and that they all passed through the sea. They were all baptized into Moses in the cloud and in the sea. They all ate the same spiritual food and drank the same spiritual drink; for they drank from the spiritual rock that accompanied them, and that rock was Christ. Nevertheless, God was not pleased with most of them; their bodies were scattered in the wilderness. Now these things occurred as examples to keep us from setting our hearts on evil things as they did (1 Corinthians 10:1-6).*

Scottish theologian Patrick Fairbairn has written extensively about the use of typology in the Bible. He defines it this way:

> *A type is a real person, place, object, or event that God ordained to act as a predictive pattern or resemblance of Jesus' person and work or opposition to both.* [16]

As we have already learned, all of creation was given to us as a way to lead us to Christ, so it is easy to see how God would, in turn, use people and events all throughout history to point to a greater reality coming in the future. Understanding the use of typology is, therefore, very helpful in reading the Old Testament.

Examples of Typology in Noah

One of the most poignant examples of typology in the Bible is the familiar story of Noah in Genesis 11. God uses this story to point us to His redemptive work on the cross to save sinners. I want us to look at four very interesting ways this story accomplishes that.

First of all, the name "Noah" actually means "rest."

Noah's father, Lamech, gave him this name. Genesis 5:29 tells us why:

> *This one will give us rest from our work and from the toil of our hands arising from the ground which the LORD has cursed.*

His reference to the curse of the ground refers back to the promise God made Adam. So Lamech is speaking prophetically not only of Noah, but also of the One who would ultimately deliver mankind from the curse of sinful disobedience. He was not only speaking of a deliverance that would come about in Noah's lifetime, but also of a future eternal deliverance that would break the cosmic curse on all mankind.

Secondly, the ark itself is a symbol of Christ.

In this passage, we learn that the water was a manifestation of the wrath of God against His disobedient and rebellious creation. The use of water for God's judgment is actually significant. At the creation event, the Lord God brought order out of chaos by separating the waters. And so water in this way represented chaos. When mankind rebelled against God, they were in the process of "de-creation." God gave them over to their rebellious ways and brought the chaos of the flood back into their lives. Those who were inside the ark escaped God's wrath and were kept dry. In a similar way, the work of Jesus on the cross "brings us in" to God's favor and secures us from the wrath and justice of God. Even the way the ark was built points to our deliverance in Christ:

> *Make for yourself an ark of gopher wood; you shall make the ark with rooms, and shall cover it inside and out with pitch (Genesis 6:14).*

The word for "cover" in Hebrew is the word "kofar," which literally means "atonement." The ark was covered inside and out with pitch, which subsequently protected the ark from the water outside. In a similar way, our lives have been atoned for by the blood of Christ, who secures us from the wrath of God (1 John 2:2). What an awesome picture of Christ's eventual work on the cross! Truly, "As it was in the days of Noah, so it will be at the coming of the Son of Man" (Matthew 24:37).

Third, there was only one door in the ark.

Genesis 6:16 tells us that God instructed Noah to put one door on the side of the ark. There was only one way in. If a person was to find salvation from the flood, there was only one way to that salvation. In the same way, the Bible teaches us that there is only one way for us to find salvation, and that is through the atoning work of Christ.

> *I am the door. If anyone enters by Me, he will be saved (John 10:9).*

> *I am the way, the truth, and the life. No one comes to the Father except through Me (John 14:6).*

But we don't just find types of Christ in the Old Testament record, we also find anti-types as well. These serve the same purpose as types but in an opposite way. Whereas a type is a positive example of a future person or event, an anti-type is a negative example. One of the most prominent demonstrations of an anti-type in Scripture is the story of the Tower of Babel found in Genesis 11.

As the story unfolds, we learn that mankind moved eastward along the plain of Shenir after the flood. It was there that they decided to build a great city to avoid being "scattered over the face of the whole earth." You may recall that God had instructed mankind to go out into all of the world, and to be fruitful, and to multiply (Genesis 1:28). In this sense, we learn that God willed for His creation to be diverse with multiple cultures, races, and languages spread out over the face of the planet.

But here all of mankind had come together and was

speaking one language. They had disobeyed God's will and were determined in their disobedience to remain one culture and language. They were developing a great tower stretching into the heavens, representing man's attempt to replace God. God was wary of their disobedience and destroyed their tower, confusing their language and forcing mankind once again to go out into the earth and develop different cultures and languages.

It was here that the "Babylonian spirit" was established. Later this city would be known as Babylon and would continue to represent a city in opposition to the purposes of God. In this sense, it is an "anti-type" of the city of God. The book of Revelation captures this concept as it continually warns God's people to come out of "Babylon," a defiled and godless city:

> *And he cried mightily with a strong voice saying, Babylon the great is fallen, is fallen, and has become the habitation of devils, and the hold of every foul spirit, and a cage of every unclean and hateful bird (Revelation 18:2).*

So it is obvious that in the book of Revelation, God's Word uses the actual historical city of Babylon as an anti-type to the city of God. In his book, *Progress of Redemption*, William Van Gemeran articulates this point very well:

> *Babel/Babylon becomes in the Bible a symbol of self-restraint, imperialistic secularism: control without*

accountability to the Creator. The spirit of secularism can co-exist with religions and deities, but not with the absolutism of the Creator-God. Humanism and secularism are bound to run counter to theism. Isaiah saw this spirit in the imperial ambitions of Assyria and Babylon (10:7-11; 14:4-6; 47:5-7, 10). John the apostle symbolically speaks of the Roman Empire and all kingdoms to follow as Babylon the Great. Babylon, the seducer of nations, kings, and merchants will fall (Revelation 18). [17]

As you can see, there is much to learn from the various types and anti-types found in Scripture. I should provide a word of caution as we move forward to look at Scripture in this way.

First of all, it is important to not be overly zealous when applying types to Old Testament passages. Not everyone or everything in Scripture is a type or anti-type of Christ! There have been many Bible teachers in the past who have abused and overstated the presence of Old Testament typology. Keep in mind, the most accurate Old Testament types are the ones that are revealed by the New Testament.

Secondly, remember that a type is limited in its scope and only points to a greater truth. The type in itself is not the ultimate truth. A type can only point one to that truth. A type only resembles the truth in some way, but is not the truth itself. Not every image or type of a future truth is perfect in its analogy. For instance, the Old Testament believer would only come to saving faith as he looked forward to the future redeemer, who is the only perfect embodiment of future redemption.

But as we will see in coming chapters, God has committed a large portion of his Scripture to the utilization of types as an effective way to reveal his redemptive plan. So there must be a very good reason for us to know and study them.

Reflect:

Read the story of Noah and the Ark in Genesis 6. Why did God send the flood? How does the flood represent the judgment and wrath of God? What does it mean that God gave them over to their sin? How is God's judgment represented by Him simply allowing the consequences of our choices to play out naturally? Do you see how this can be a form of His judgment? What does this say to us about His grace? How does the cross of Christ accomplish the same thing as the ark?

Nine: Abraham and Isaac Point Us to Jesus

By faith Abraham, when called to go to a place he would later receive as his inheritance, obeyed and went, even though he did not know where he was going. By faith he made his home in the Promised Land like a stranger in a foreign country; he lived in tents, as did Isaac and Jacob, who were heirs with him of the same promise. For he was looking forward to the city with foundations, whose architect and builder is God (Hebrews 11:8-10).

One of the things I like to tell my congregation is that Jesus is on every page, every paragraph, and every line of the Bible from Genesis to Revelation. What do I mean by this? The Bible is really only about one thing—and that one thing is the story of God's redemption of mankind. This is the "meta-narrative" of the entire Bible.

Connecting Your Story to a Bigger Story

I recently heard a lecture by C.S. Lewis biographer, Alistair McGrath, recounting the influence of J.R.R. Tolkien (author of *Lord of the Rings*) on Lewis. It was Tolkien who was most influential on Lewis' conversion to Christianity from atheism. McGrath made a statement that resonates strongly here. He said that Tolkien told Lewis that it was best to look at Christianity as a story. "You will never find true meaning in life unless you can connect your story to a bigger story that is outside yourself." [18]

He told him that when you read the Bible, you need to see it is a story that happened in real history, and that it helps us to connect to life's true meaning. According to McGrath, this was the point that resonated most effectively with Lewis. C.S Lewis would later write:

> *Good stories don't say 'look at me,' they says 'look through me' to see the bigger point.* [19]

Once a person gets that truth about Scripture distilled down into his or her heart, it is really not that hard to see that Jesus indeed is in every line of the stories we read in the Old Testament.

I like the way Professor Bryan Chappel explains the concept:

> *You do not explain what an acorn is, even if you say many true things about it (e.g., it is brown, has a cap, is found on the ground, is gathered by squirrels), if you do not in some way relate it to an oak tree. In a similar sense, students of the Bible cannot properly explain a seed (or portion) of biblical revelation, even if they say many true things about it, unless they relate it to the redeeming work of God that all Scripture ultimately purposes to disclose. In this sense, the entire Bible is Christ-centered because His redemptive work in all its incarnational, atoning, rising, interceding, and reigning dimensions is the capstone of all of God's revelation*

and His dealings with His people. Thus, no aspect of revelation can be thoroughly understood or explained in isolation from some aspect of God's redeeming work. [20]

Just as one does not talk about an acorn without relating it back to the great oak tree it fell from, one does not look at any line in Scripture without relating it back to the bigger story it fell from, and that bigger story is the redemptive narrative of almighty God in the person of Jesus Christ.

So as we continue along our journey of reading through the Old Testament and finding how it points us to the coming of Jesus, we should keep in mind that all that we are reading is trying to say something to us about God's ultimate plan. This is especially evident as we read the stories about the four men in the book of Genesis who are known collectively as "the patriarchs." These four men are Abraham, Isaac, Jacob, and Joseph. They are known as the patriarchs because it was through their offspring that Israel was formed. God in His grace chose Abraham to be the "father of many nations," and so it was his progeny that produced God's chosen people and ultimately brought about the birth of Christ.

But there are many other ways that the life of Abraham points us to Christ. We will deal later with the covenant that God established with Abraham, so I will not belabor that point. I will instead focus on other stories within his life that are significant.

Abraham

Abraham was a man of faith, the eight times great-grandson of Noah, who was living in a place called Ur in Mesopotamia when he heard the call of God to go to Canaan and claim his inheritance. Here we learn that God singled out Abraham and chose him for a special task that would have great historical and even eternal significance. Whereas the Lord God chose Noah and the entire human race suffered, in this case the Lord God chose Abraham, and the entire human race received a blessing.

So he left the place of his birth and obeyed God. In spite of many hardships along the way, Abraham persisted in his journey, and God made him a promise that he would be the father of many offspring. He told him that his children would be as many as the stars in the sky, and that his seed would be a blessing to many nations.

Of course, this would be the eventual nation of Israel whose various tribes were descendants of Abraham's grandson, Jacob. That line of descendants would carry great importance to the nation of Israel down through time. When the Israelites were oppressed in Egypt. it was said that God "remembered His promise to Abraham and had mercy on them" (Exodus 2:24). In the book of Nehemiah, Ezra's prayer also illustrates this:

You are the LORD God, who chose Abram and brought

him out of Ur of the Chaldeans and named him Abraham (Nehemiah 9:7).

These and many other examples throughout the Old Testament reveal how vitally important it was to the Israelites to identify with Abraham and his promise from God. They often referred to themselves as the children of Abraham, Isaac, and Jacob.

That promise to Abraham figures prominently in the New Testament Scriptures as well and is a very important clue to the eventual birth of Christ. In fact, the Bible teaches that anyone who is in Christ is a part of the "seed of Abraham." Paul the apostle put it like this:

The promises were spoken to Abraham and to his seed. Scripture does not say "and to seeds," meaning many people, but "and to your seed," meaning one person, who is Christ. What I mean is this: The law, introduced 430 years later, does not set aside the covenant previously established by God and thus do away with the promise. For if the inheritance depends on the law, then it no longer depends on the promise; but God in his grace gave it to Abraham through a promise (Galatians 3:16-18).

So how can it be that any person who follows Christ is a descendant of Abraham? The answer is that the promise to Abraham was very specific. Paul's point in this passage is that although Abraham's offspring would eventually become the chosen people of Israel, that the real thrust of the promise was that out of that nation would come the Anointed One, the redeemer of all mankind, Jesus Christ. This is why Paul makes the point that the promise was for a singular "seed," not for a plural "seeds."

But Paul also makes the further point that people who commit to Christ are children of Abraham because they are "children of promise." So what does it mean to be a child of promise?

We learn the answer in an explanation of the two sons of Abraham. Because he was impatient and did not believe God could give him a child through his elderly wife, Sarah, Abraham took matters into his own hands and had his first son Ishmael. This did not come about through the promise of God, but through his own disbelief and impatience. Ishmael was born to his servant, Hagar.

His second son was Isaac, who was miraculously conceived by Sarah out of faith and obedience rather than by disbelief and works. So it can be said that one of Abraham's sons was the offspring of works, while the other was the offspring of promise, or faith.

Paul builds the point that this is a picture of our faith. He points out that we come to Christ not by our works, but by our faith. And it is this kind of faith of Abraham that we are to "inherit" as a result of our belief in Jesus. Paul makes this point in Romans 4:

> *What then shall we say that Abraham, our forefather according to the flesh, discovered in this matter?*

If, in fact, Abraham was justified by works, he had something to boast about—but not before God. What does Scripture say? "Abraham believed God, and it was credited to him as righteousness."

Now to the one who works, wages are not credited as a gift but as an obligation. However, to the one who does not work but trusts God who justifies the ungodly, their faith is credited as righteousness (Romans 4:1-4).

What was credited to Abraham as righteousness? Many people mistakenly believe that Paul is saying that faith itself becomes righteousness, but that is not what he is saying. Instead, he is saying that our faith joins us with Christ, and it is Christ who is our righteousness. In the same way that Abraham and Sarah did not produce the child of promise without God's supernatural intervention, you and I can only receive God's righteousness by the miraculous work of Christ through faith.

The famous 16th-century Baptist theologian, John Bunyon, says this:

One day as I was passing into the field . . . this sentence fell upon my soul. Thy righteousness is in heaven. And me thought, withal, I saw with the eyes of my soul Jesus Christ at God's right hand; there, I say, was my righteousness; so that wherever I was, or whatever I was doing, God could not say of me, he wants [lacks] my righteousness, for that was just before [in front of] him. I also saw, moreover, that it was not my good frame of heart that made my righteousness better, nor yet my bad frame that made my righteousness worse, for my righteousness was Jesus Christ himself, "The same yesterday, today and, forever." Now did my chains fall off my legs indeed. I was loosed from my afflictions and irons; my temptations also fled away; so that from that time those dreadful Scriptures of God left off to trouble me; now went I also home rejoicing for the grace and love of God. [21]

What a great picture of our salvation! But the stories that connect the life of Abraham to Jesus do not end there.

In Genesis 14, we read how Abraham and some of his men facilitated a daring rescue of his nephew Lot, who had been taken captive by King Kedorlaomer of Elam. On their way back, they encountered a very interesting man named Melchizedek.

What made Melchizedek so interesting is that he was both a king and a "priest of the Most High God." That terminology, the "Most High God," is distinguished from the Jewish term for God which is "Yahweh." This means that Melchizedek was not a priest in the Jewish sense (priests in Judaism were descendants of Aaron), but was a priest in a more universal sense. The Bible says he blessed Abraham, and that Abraham gave him a tithe.

The reason this is important is that over 2,000 years would go by before Melchizedek is ever mentioned again. He is not mentioned by any of the prophets, judges, priests, or poets of the Old Testament. He is only mentioned again in the New Testament in Hebrews 4 where the Bible says that Jesus Christ is a priest "in the order of Melchizedek."

Scripture is making the point that Jesus was a priest not only for Israel, but for the nations. It is saying that Jesus is our ultimate mediator who goes to the Father on our behalf. He is both our king and our priest. In this way, Hebrews is teaching us that this remote character from the book of Genesis, who takes up a mere three verses in a kind of side story in the life of Abraham, was placed in our biblical consciousness as a way to foreshadow someone who would come 2,000 years later!

Truly, He was the long-expected Jesus.

The writer of the book of Hebrews saw how prominently father Abraham figured into Christian faith in another way as well. He wrote this:

> *By faith Abraham, when God tested him, offered Isaac as a sacrifice. He who had embraced the promises was about to sacrifice his one and only son, even though God had said to him, "It is through Isaac that your offspring will be reckoned." Abraham reasoned that God could even raise the dead, and so in a manner of speaking he did receive Isaac back from death (Hebrews 11:17-19).*

This brings us to our next example of how Christ was foreshadowed in Scripture, through the life of Isaac, who was the son of Abraham.

Isaac

Isaac was the son of promise to Abraham and Rebekah. When the angel of the Lord first told the aging couple that they would have a son, Rebekah actually laughed out loud. When the Lord fulfilled His promise and the baby was born, they named him "Isaac," which means "laughter" (Genesis 21:6).

As we have already seen, Isaac was actually the younger son of Abraham, in that Sarah's hand-maiden, Hagar, had given birth to Ishmael. Remember that Romans 4 tells us that this situation with Ishmael and Isaac is actually an object lesson for our faith. One was born out of man's desire to take matters in his own hands (works), and the other was born out of God's faithfulness and promise (grace). So the story of Isaac's birth is in this way a foreshadowing of the redemption that God would bring into our lives.

But there is another way the birth of Isaac foreshadows Christ, and that is in the order of his birth. Isaac was the second son of Abraham, and in this sense he would not have realized all of the privileges of primogeniture, and thus, inheritance from his father. Primogeniture was the normal practice of ancient Israel in which all of the family wealth was passed to the oldest son. But because Ishmael was not born of Sarah, he was eventually cast out, and in this way Isaac received the status of first and only son.

It is interesting to note that very often in Scripture this theme of the younger son gaining inheritance is prominent. Abel was the younger son whose sacrifice was favored; Isaac was the younger son but received the inheritance; Jacob was the younger son but attained the birthright; Joseph was the younger son but received the coat and eventually saved Israel; David was the younger son who slew Goliath and became king. This theme of the younger son is emphasized repeatedly.

There has to be something to this recurring theme of a younger son receiving the inheritance. Of course the answer is that it points to the eventual Messiah. Jesus Himself is the second Adam. After the first Adam squandered his inheritance (in this case the garden), the second Adam, Jesus, has come and restored our standing with God. So do you see how even the order of Isaac's birth gives us a clue of the future redeemer?

But the foreshadowing in the life of Isaac does not stop there. The most famous event in Isaac's life actually took place on top of Mt. Moriah, a place of great later significance. God told Abraham to sacrifice his one and only son Isaac on that mountain.

Think of the significance of this event. Abraham is to sacrifice his one and only son, a son miraculously born and completely innocent, on top of a hill.

Does that sound familiar?

Do you remember at the beginning of the book that I made the point that the Old Testament makes a lot more sense when you read it from the perspective of the Gospel? If you understand that the Bible is a love story about God's redemption, then all the other stories fit into that theme. This is one of those times when the story only makes sense when you put it in the context of Jesus dying on the cross for our sin.

So let's continue our story. Abraham and Isaac are making their way up the hill when Isaac says to his father, "Father, where is the sacrifice?" Abraham's answer was one for the ages. He said,

> *The Lord God will provide the sacrifice (Genesis 22:8).*

The parallels of the sacrifice of Isaac to the sacrifice of Christ are stark and undeniable:

- Abraham took Isaac all the way to Mount Moriah—to the very mountain range of the later crucifixion of Jesus.
- After three days, Abraham "lifted up his eyes" and saw Moriah.
- God told Abraham, "Take your son, your one and only son, whom you love."
- Isaac carried his own wood to the place of sacrifice.
- Isaac willingly offered his life as a sacrifice.

Truly, this is a passage that ought to be highlighted and underlined in every Bible. It is, in fact, the major theme of all of Scripture. This is one of those passages that gives me goose bumps when I think about how God orchestrated all of the events on that ancient hill many hundreds of years before the time of Jesus as a way to tell the story that would resonate in the hearts of future believers.

But the story doesn't end there. As Abraham was preparing Isaac to be sacrificed, God provided a ram, a perfect sacrifice.

The significance of this foreshadowing of the Gospel was not lost on the early believers. Shortly after writing this chapter, I made a trip into the catacombs in Rome, where over 500,000 second and third-century Christians were buried outside the Roman gates. This historical site is truly inspiring, as it is a physical representation of the tens of thousands of early believers who made the ultimate sacrifice for their faith. The imagery painted on the walls provides fascinating glimpses into the teaching of the early church before the time of Constantine.

I was fascinated by one particular fresco above the crypt of a third-century martyr. The image in the fresco was of Abraham and Isaac standing before the altar with a ram standing next to them, their arms outstretched toward God rejoicing over God's provision of a sacrifice. The painting was in an array of other significant biblical images such as the Lord's Supper and the resurrection. As I stood there considering the meaning of that early fresco painted just a few generations after the time of Christ, I was in awe of the thought that these early Christians integrated this story of Abraham and Isaac into their biblical teaching of the Gospel.

The catacombs in Rome are indisputable evidence that from the very beginning of the church, Christians have seen the expectation of Jesus in the first testament.

It is hard to imagine a more poignant example of an Old Testament story that points us to Jesus. In fact, I believe Jesus Himself uses this story as an example in a discussion with some Jewish teachers who were confronting Him about His teaching about eternal life. The Jewish teachers had just finished making the point that even their father, Abraham, had tasted death. They said to him, surely you don't think you are better than father Abraham?

Jesus answered them somewhat cryptically,

> *Abraham rejoiced to see my day (Genesis 8:56).*

What could Jesus have meant by that statement? We all know that Abraham lived 2,000 years before the time of Jesus. So how could he have rejoiced about His day?

The famous Bible scholar, F.F. Bruce, gives the answer:

> *I believe the most attractive answer is that Jesus was talking about the sacrifice of Isaac.* [22]

In other words, Abraham rejoiced about his son being

spared. He rejoiced that there was a better sacrifice. He rejoiced because the sparing of his son was a foreshadowing of a time to come in which the Son of God would not be spared. Abraham's one and only son was spared, but on another hill in another time, God's only son would lay down His life on the altar. Instead of the hand of sacrifice being held back, God would allow it to come down on His only Son, and Jesus would receive the blow.

That is how Abraham would have rejoiced to see the day of Jesus.

Reflect:

Read Hebrews 11:8-12. As Christians, we are "children of the promise" in that we come to faith in Christ in the same way Abraham trusted God to fulfill His promise. What does it mean to you that you have been saved by His grace rather than by your works? Why do you believe the story of the sacrifice of Isaac is so important to our understanding of the cross?

Ten: Jacob and Joseph Lead Us to Jesus

Are you greater than our father Jacob, who gave us the well and drank from it himself, as did also his sons and his livestock? (Woman at the well, to Jesus in John 4:12)

John Newton was born the son of an English merchant marine captain in 1705. His mother was a devoted Christian who diligently taught him her faith until her untimely death when he was only seven-years-old. Now left under the complete influence of a father who had no interest in Christianity, his life took a trajectory far from God. Newton was a restless and unsettled soul who tended toward heavy drinking and compulsive behavior. He was neither a good sailor, nor a good soldier. In his youth he was undisciplined, disrespectful, and out of control.

It was therefore inevitable that Newton would spend more time below deck in the brig of a navy ship than up above on duty after joining a British navy frigate. He was arrogant, morally devoid of character, and would later write, "I made it my study to tempt and seduce others." [23] This pattern continued until he finally talked his captain into putting him aboard a slave ship in exchange for his confinement. The captain was more than happy to oblige in order to be rid of him.

It was here that John Newton's life descended into a new kind of darkness.

Slave ships of the 18th century were like sailing hell-holes. One eye witness called them the "cargo of the living dead." Here is more of that account:

The heat of these horrid places was so great and the odor so offensive that it was quite impossible to enter them, even had there been room. They were measured as above when the slaves had left them. The officers insisted that the poor suffering creatures should be admitted on deck to get air and water. This was opposed by the mate of the slaver, who, from a feeling that they deserved it, declared they would murder them all.

The officers, however, persisted, and the poor beings were all turned up together. It is impossible to conceive the effect of this eruption—517 fellow creatures of all ages and sexes, some children, some adults, some old men and women, all in a state of total nudity, scrambling out together to taste the luxury of a little fresh air and water. They came swarming up like bees from the aperture of a hive till the whole deck was crowded to suffocation front stem to stern, so that it was impossible to imagine where they could all have come from or how they could have been stowed away. On looking into the places where they had been crammed, there were found some children next to the sides of the ship, in the places most remote from light and air; they were lying nearly in a torpid state after the rest had turned out. The little creatures seemed indifferent as to life or death, and when they were carried on deck, many of them could not stand.

After enjoying for a short time the unusual luxury of air, some water was brought; it was then that the extent of their sufferings was exposed in a fearful manner. They all rushed like maniacs toward it. No entreaties or threats or blows could restrain them; they shrieked and struggled and fought with one another for a drop of this precious liquid, as if they grew rabid at the sight of it. [24]

It was in these deplorable conditions that Newton spent his next three years. His clothes soon turned to rags, and he was forced to beg for his food. It wasn't until his transfer to another ship that Newton's life began to brighten.

Those dark days had sparked a flame of his mother's witness. On the new ship, he was given a copy of Thomas A. Merton's *Imitation of Christ*, and his life slowly turned. A sober Newton took on more and more responsibility and was finally transferred to an office in London. It was here that he became a full-blown follower of Jesus and later an influential pastor in London. Sickened by what he had seen in the slave trade, Newton became the spiritual mentor to William Wilberforce, who led England to end slavery for good.

He was also the one who famously penned these words;

Amazing grace how sweet the sound
That saved a wretch like me
I once was lost but now I'm found
'Twas blind but now I see.

The lesson of the life of John Newton is that God can take broken pieces and turn them into something beautiful. There is no more stark example of this in the Old Testament than the life of Jacob. A man, who like Newton, began his adult life tempting, seducing, and cheating the people around him. But as we will find out, God took that morally corrupt life and used it for His glory.

Jacob

From the very beginning of his life, Jacob was a deceiver. The Bible teaches that Jacob was actually a twin who was born immediately after his brother Esau. But because Jacob had a hold of Esau's heel when he was born, his parents named him "heel snatcher," or "Ja-cob" in Hebrew. And it was an apt name, because Jacob was always tripping up people.

Jacob lived a very interesting life, and many of his stories have very compelling spiritual themes. But for our purposes, I want us to focus on one story in particular. In Genesis 28, the Bible describes a time when Jacob falls asleep and has a dream. In the dream, he sees a ladder that is stretched into the heavens, and angels are ascending and descending. The Lord God repeats the promise He has made to Jacob's grandfather, Abraham, that He will make him a father of many nations. Jacob wakes up and says, "Surely the presence of the Lord is in this place, and I knew it not." Jacob then set up a marker to commemorate the spot where he had the dream.

Maybe you are thinking, "That was an interesting story about Jacob's dream, but how does it point us to Jesus?"

The answer is found in the first chapter of the Gospel of John. Jesus is calling together his future disciples, and he comes upon a man named Nathaniel. Read the account of how Jesus meets this future disciple:

> *When Jesus saw Nathaniel approaching, he said of him, "Here truly is an Israelite in whom there is no deceit."*
>
> *"How do you know me?" Nathanael asked.*
>
> *Jesus answered, "I saw you while you were still under the fig tree before Philip called you."*
>
> *Then Nathanael declared, "Rabbi, you are the Son of God; you are the king of Israel."*
>
> *Jesus said, "You believe because I told you I saw you under the fig tree. You will see greater things than that." He then added, "Very truly I tell you, you will see 'heaven open, and the angels of God ascending and descending on' the Son of Man" (John 1:47-50).*

Why was Nathaniel so blown away by this first meeting with Jesus that he would suddenly declare that Jesus is the Son of God? It could only mean that Jesus had so laid bear the heart of Nathaniel that he was convinced that He was the Messiah. I believe that Nathaniel very well could have been reading Genesis 28 when Jesus saw him under the fig tree. I believe the evidence of this is Jesus' reference to that Scripture in verse 51.

But what does it mean for Jesus to say that as Nathaniel follows him, he will see heaven open, and angels ascending and descending? There is only one possible answer, and that is that through the work of Christ, a true ladder will be produced that will allow God's people to have complete access to heaven. I have an idea that Nathaniel was praying and meditating on the meaning of the ladder when Jesus saw him. I have a sense that he was considering how the ladder might even be the Son of Man, the future Messiah. I wonder as I read this passage if perhaps Jesus knew what Nathaniel had been thinking and seized on that thought as he called him to be His disciple. It was as if Jesus was saying, "I'm the One you have been looking for!"

Jesus is the ladder that Jacob saw in his dream. And it was Jacob's dream that leads us to the long-awaited Jesus.

Jacob lived a good long life with many sons, and it was those sons who formed the lineage for the nation of Israel and its twelve tribes. At the end of his life, Jacob called all of his sons together and gave them a blessing, and that blessing became the prophetic imperative for each of those tribes. It was the tribe of Judah that brought about the earthly parentage of Jesus.

Judah was the tribe of kings, and Levi was the tribe of priests. One could not be a priest unless he was a descendant from Levi. Jesus was an exception as He was a priest in the order of Melchizedek. And so it was prophetically significant that Jesus' line was from Judah to David to Joseph, for as the book of Hebrews tells us, He was prophet, priest, and king. Remember that it was because Joseph, the step-father of Jesus, was of the tribe of King David that he and Mary made the trip to the "City of David" (Bethlehem), where Jesus was born.

And so you can see that the stories of the patriarchs are incredibly significant to the foreshadowing of Jesus. Now you know why Matthew began his Gospel account of the life of Jesus by starting with His lineage.

Imagine how the disciples on the road to Emmaus must have marveled at all that Jesus told them about what the Old Testament Scriptures revealed about the coming Messiah. Think of all the connections we have already found, and we are not yet out of the account of the patriarchs. Before we leave our patriarchal journey, we need to visit the most famous great-grandson of Abraham and son of Jacob, the indelible commander of Egypt, Joseph.

Joseph

One of the most colorful and important stories in all the Old Testament is the story of the eleventh son of Jacob. Joseph was the favored son of Jacob who drew the resentment of his older brothers. Out of that resentment, they feigned his death and sold him into slavery. The slave traders subsequently took Joseph away from the land of

Canaan and into the foreign kingdom of Egypt. Through an amazing array of circumstances, Joseph rose from slave and prisoner to be the second in command under Pharaoh of all of Egypt. It is hard to imagine a more meteoric rise in power than that of a lowly Hebrew slave to the highest seat in the greatest military power in the world. It was the influence and power of Joseph that preserved the family of Jacob and secured the future of the nation of Israel.

The life of Joseph is one of the most recognized in all of the Bible. It has even inspired a Hollywood blockbuster and a Broadway musical! But what makes the story of Joseph truly remarkable is the sheer number of ways his life foreshadows the life of Jesus. Some biblical scholars claim that the life of Joseph has over 100 parallels to the life of Jesus. Here is a small sampling of how his life compares to Jesus:

> Joseph was a good shepherd (Genesis 37:2; John 10:11).

> He was beloved by his father (Genesis 37:3; Matthew 3).

> He was sent by his father to look for his lost brothers (Genesis 37:14; Luke 20:13).

> He was accused of crimes he did not commit (Genesis 37:18; Luke 23:21).

> His was stripped of his clothing (Genesis 37:23; Matthew 27:28).

> He was sold by his own for silver coins (Genesis 37:28; Matthew 26:15).

- > He descended into the pit (Genesis 37:24; Matthew 12:40).
- > He rose again from the pit (Genesis 37:28; 1 Corinthians 15:4).
- > His imprisonment and slavery resulted in the liberation of his family (Genesis 45:3; Romans 11:26).
- > He was tempted but did not give in (Genesis 39:17; Matthew 26:60).
- > He was put in prison with two other prisoners (Genesis 39:20; Luke 23:43).
- > He was exalted after suffering (Genesis 41:14; Philippians 2:9).
- > He forgave those who sinned against him (Genesis 42:6; Matthew 24:21).
- > He said about his oppressors, "You meant it for evil, but God meant it for good" (Genesis 45:3; Romans 11:26).
- > He forgave those who wronged him and brought them into a new land (Genesis 45; Romans 11).
- > He began as a suffering servant and finished as exalted king (Genesis 41; Revelation 19:16).

It is truly amazing to think about all the ways the stories of the patriarchs point us to Christ. From Abraham to Isaac to Jacob to Joseph, there can be no denying that God gave us these stories to help us understand the meaning of the most important story of all. If you think about it, there really is only one story that resonates in the human heart, and that is the story of miraculous redemption out of the pit of despair. I believe that every other good story will have elements of that one truly great story. The story of our redemption is the great oak from which every other story falls.

Jesus is the true and better Abraham...the true and better Isaac...the true and better Jacob...the true and better Joseph!

That is what the majority of the book of Genesis says to us. But our journey does not stop here with the patriarchs and the book of Genesis. In some ways it is just the beginning. For the most significant and important analogy of the work of salvation on our behalf was foreshadowed in the Old Testament in the amazing sequence of events that came to be known as "Pesach" or "Passover." That is the subject of the next chapter.

Reflect:

The stories of Jacob and Joseph both involve serious failing on the part of God's people. What do you think it means that God has used flawed and sinful people in order to carry out His designs and purposes for creation? What does it say about His grace? What does it say about how He can use you?

Eleven: Let My People Go!

> *By faith Moses, when he had grown up, refused to be known as the son of Pharaoh's daughter. He chose to be mistreated along with the people of God rather than to enjoy the fleeting pleasures of sin. He regarded disgrace for the sake of Christ as of greater value than the treasures of Egypt, because he was looking ahead to his reward. By faith he left Egypt, not fearing the king's anger; he persevered because he saw him who is invisible. By faith he kept the Passover and the application of blood, so that the destroyer of the firstborn would not touch the firstborn of Israel (Hebrews 11:24-28).*

Through several decades in Egypt after the time of Joseph, fortunes began to change for the displaced people of God. Within about seventy years of the death of Joseph, the Israelites were a despised race in Egypt, and Pharaoh forced them into slave labor. The Hebrew people cried out to God for deliverance, and God heard their prayers through the life of one of the most memorable people in history. This was a man who went from being a prince to an avenger to a runaway, and eventually the great law-giver and spiritual leader of the nation of Israel. Of course I am talking about Moses.

How Moses is a "Type of Christ"

There are many aspects of the life of Moses that foreshadow the life of Christ, but none are near as significant as the exodus event.

The familiar story begins when Moses went to the mighty Pharaoh with a message from the Lord, "Let my people go!" And of course, Moses didn't just have the words of God behind him, he also had the mighty works of God. Through various plagues, increasing in intensity and effect, God brought about the necessary pressure onto Pharaoh. The final plague was the death angel who took the first-born son of every family in Egypt that did not have the blood of the lamb sprinkled on their doorpost. The gruesome symbolism of that final plague is one of the most powerful markers of redemptive history that would eventually come to be celebrated as "Passover."

Of course, the use of those plagues was very effective, and eventually Pharaoh succumbed to the demands of Yahweh through His servant Moses. This led to the famous exodus in which an entire people group fled the land of Egypt and crossed the Red Sea to begin their journey back to their Promised Land in Canaan.

The subsequent escape from Egypt was one that figured very profoundly into the religious life of Judaism and into the consciousness of Christian doctrine. The Passover itself was a celebration of the "passing over" of the death angel for every Israelite who was covered by the blood of the lamb. It was at the Passover meal that Jesus inaugurated a new Christian tradition that we call "The Lord's Supper." It was at that meal that Jesus revealed Himself to be the fulfillment of the Passover. It was by His work and by His blood that humankind found redemption. He was the ultimate Passover. His body was the bread, and His blood was symbolized in the cup of wine. He was the lamb slain for the sins of the world.

Tim Keller of Redeemer Presbyterian in New York City tells how the story of Passover opened his eyes to the incredible unity of Scripture and profound meaning of redemptive history. At a "Together for the Gospel" event several years ago, he said this about something that happened to him early in his ministry:

> *If there is one Old Testament passage that the New Testament invites us to read in a Christ-centered way as a paradigm of Christ's salvation, it's the exodus. I'll never forget nearly forty years ago sitting in R. C. Sproul's living room in Stahlstown, Pennsylvania. Alec Motyer, a British Old Testament scholar I had never heard of, was visiting. I was on the floor with a bunch of other college and seminary students, and Sproul said to Motyer, "Tell us about the connection between the Old and New Testaments." Motyer replied something like this: Think about it. Think of what an Israelite would say on the way to Canaan after passing through the Red Sea. If you asked an Israelite, "Who are you?" he might reply, "I*

was in a foreign land under the sentence of death and in bondage, but I took shelter under the blood of the lamb. And our mediator led us out, and we crossed over. Now we're on our way to the Promised Land, though we're not there yet. But he has given us his law to make us a community, and he has given us a tabernacle because we must live by grace and forgiveness. And he is present in our midst, and he will stay with us until we arrive home. Then Motyer added, "That's exactly what a Christian says—almost word for word." And my twenty-three-year-old self thought, "Huh." [25]

So as you can see, there is a profound connection to be made between the exodus event and our salvation in Jesus Christ. A book about the "long-expected Jesus" would not be complete unless adequate time was spent making that connection. So I would like for us to think about all of the ways these two things are connected, and why it is important.

First of all, the Passover event relates to our salvation because through salvation in Christ, we have been released from bondage.

Salvation is about getting out of bondage. In fact, the word "redemption" means to get out of debt. And that is literally what happened to the Israelites. They were slaves in Egypt. By the effective negotiations with Pharaoh on Israel's behalf, the Lord God set them free from their debt of bondage.

It wasn't long before the Egyptians realized what a great deal they had with so many slaves to do their work, and so they changed their minds. They decided to pursue the Israelites to either kill or recapture them. It was then that the Bible says the Israelites began to grumble against Moses. Remarkably, many of them wanted to remain in captivity. "It would have been better if we had stayed in Egypt and died," they said.

Why in the world would anyone want to stay in bondage and slavery? I can't imagine anyone being set free, regretting that they had made that choice, and wanting to go right back into bondage.

But isn't that exactly what we do? We have acceptance, renewed status, eternal security, and salvation in Christ, and yet we continue to go back to the bondage of our sinful condition. We go back into our feelings of guilt, inadequacy, and sinful habits. And yet in Christ, we have been liberated from those slave masters. They no longer have a hold on us, yet our flesh keeps pulling us back. One of my favorite C.S. Lewis quotes relates to this very truth:

> *It would seem that Our Lord finds our desires not too strong, but too weak. We are half-hearted creatures, fooling about with drink and sex and ambition when infinite joy is offered us, like an ignorant child who wants to go on making mud pies in a slum because he cannot imagine what is meant by the offer of a holiday at the sea. We are far too easily pleased.*[26]

Our salvation relates to the exodus because, in both cases, we have been set free. Sadly, we are also a lot like the Israelites in that we keep wanting back into bondage.

Secondly, our salvation relates to the exodus event because, like the exodus, it has been miraculously accomplished for us.

Just like our salvation, the exodus was accomplished for the Israelites without them having to lift a finger. Moses was their mediator, God brought the plagues, directed the words of Moses, and defended His people against the mighty Egyptian army. When the Israelites were cornered by the Egyptians at the Red Sea, it was God alone who parted the waters and opened up the way for them.

This image gives us a very powerful metaphor for our salvation. Only in Christianity is there this kind of teaching on the nature of Gods' sovereign grace. The Bible teaches that our salvation is accomplished by Jesus' work and nothing more.

It is Jesus plus nothing else.

No other religion teaches that a person is so utterly changed by the work of God, and none of it is brought about by man's work. His grace operates by crossing over. Once the Israelite crossed to the other side, there was no way for the Egyptian army to get to them. On one side they were in bondage, and on the other side they were completely free.

And that is how salvation works. In one moment one is a slave, and in the next moment he is free. At one moment, one is in bondage, and the next moment, he is liberated. One moment, one is in darkness, and the next he is in the light. One moment, one is lost, the next moment, one is found. Jesus said it like this:

> *Very truly I tell you, whoever hears my word and believes him who sent me has eternal life and will not be judged but has crossed over from death to life (John 5:24).*

Just like the exodus, our salvation in Christ is a "crossing over." I love how Isaiah the prophet states it:

> *Was it not you who dried up the sea,*
> *the waters of the great deep,*
> *who made a road in the depths of the sea*
> *so that the redeemed might cross over (Isaiah 51:10).*

His redeeming work is about crossing over. That is what salvation looks like. There is nothing we do to earn our own salvation. Like the Israelites who had varying degrees of trust in what God was doing when they crossed the sea, our salvation is not found in the degree of our belief, but only in what He has done for us. We do not merit it on our own. It is only accomplished by His work.

Again, this is what separates Christianity from every other religion. Every other religion says that we have to do these things, these works, these steps or whatever so that we can be brought into salvation. But Christianity says, "We do these

things because of what Christ has already done for us."
Our salvation is foreshadowed by the exodus, because in both cases, it is accomplished without merit.

A third and final manner in which our salvation is like the exodus is that in both, there is a mediator.

One of the most important aspects of our salvation is the fact that we have a mediator who stands in our place.

In the case of the Israelites in Egypt, Moses stood before Pharaoh and pled their case. It is important to remember that they had absolutely no authority, leverage, or ability to plead their own case. Moses spoke for God on their behalf, and it was his mediation that brought about their eventual liberation from slavery.

Moses stretched out his staff, and the Lord God brought about the plagues. Remember in Noah's time how the waters of the flood represented a picture of the judgment and wrath of God? It was a picture of a kind of "de-creation" event in which God allowed the chaos of man's sin to be exposed. At creation, God brought order out of chaos by separating the waters, and in his judgment, he allowed the waters to descend onto mankind.

Tim Keller has suggested that the plagues in Exodus are another example of this kind of judgment. These plagues were examples of God allowing man's sinful condition to manifest into a kind of "de-creation" as in the time of Noah.

With the Egyptian army at their back and the Red Sea before them, Moses stretched out his staff. God, working through Moses, drew back the sea, and Israel walked through. As the Egyptian army pursued them, the waters closed down onto them in another visual manifestation of His divine judgment. Moses was a mediator in that he represented God to His people and represented the people of Israel to the Lord God.

But there was a better mediator to come! All of these events are vivid pictures of the future mediation of Christ. Paul says this in 1 Timothy:

> *For there is one God and one mediator between God and mankind, the man Christ Jesus (1 Timothy 2:5).*

Complaining in the Desert

As Moses led the children of Israel into the desert and toward the Promised Land, one would have thought that they would have moved forward with joy and anticipation of their new-found freedom and the land of milk and honey God had promised them. But that was not the case. The biblical account of their time in the wilderness is one of continual complaining and even outright rebellion against God. Recall how we explored how the Israelites' rebellion against God in the wilderness resulted in the curse of poisonous snakes? This was one of many examples of the mediation of Moses prefiguring Christ.
Moses' mediation would be tested again and again.

One of these encounters provides another stark example of foreshadowing our salvation in Christ. We find the story in Exodus 17 where the children of Israel are suffering from thirst and are complaining to Moses that it would have been better to stay in Egypt than to suffer such thirst in the wilderness.

> *But the people were thirsty for water there, and they grumbled against Moses. They said, "Why did you bring us up out of Egypt to make us and our children and livestock die of thirst?"(Exodus 17:3)*

At this point, Moses mediates for the Israelites and cries out to the Lord God:

> *Then Moses cried out to the Lord, "What am I to do with these people? They are almost ready to stone me" (Exodus 17:4).*

The language in this complaint seems to indicate that the people of Israel are desiring to put Moses on trial for the crime of setting them free from Egypt and bringing them into the desert to fend for themselves. But the Lord God has a very interesting and emphatic answer:

> *The Lord answered Moses, "Go out in front of the people. Take with you some of the elders of Israel and take in your hand the staff with which you struck the Nile, and go" (Exodus 17:5).*

God's reply to Moses seems to be, "My people want a trial,

I will give them a trial." He tells Moses to gather the elders and to take up his staff. When God tells Moses to take hold of his staff, it normally means that the judgment of the Lord is about to be meted out! At this point, if you are following the drama of the biblical account in real time, you might be wondering, "Who will be on the receiving end of God's judgment? Moses? The Israelites?" It would be neither:

> *I will stand there before you by the rock at Horeb. Strike the rock, and water will come out of it for the people to drink (Exodus 17:6).*

Remarkably, it was the Lord God Himself who stood on the rock of judgment! He would take that sentence Himself. His instruction to Moses while His presence was on the rock was, "Strike the rock."

This sequence calls to mind another day of judgment in which the people of God stood guilty before their mediator, and the staff of God's judgment came down. But it was not the people of God who were to take the blow, but God Himself! It was only after the rock was struck that life-giving water flowed out, and the people's thirst was quenched.

From ancient times, the Jew has celebrated the time in the wilderness when the Lord God showed favor on his people and caused water to come out of the rock. It is called "Sukkot" or "Feast of the Tabernacles." There is an account in Scripture of Jesus watching people leaving that celebration. What He says to the crowd is instructive:

On the last and greatest day of the festival, Jesus stood and said in a loud voice, "Let anyone who is thirsty come to me and drink. Whoever believes in me, as Scripture has said, rivers of living water will flow from within them" (John 7:37-38).

Jesus is the one who has stood in our place.
He is the one who took the blow.
He is the "rock struck."
He is the One from whom "rivers of living water" flow!

Reflect:

Read Hebrews 11:24-28. How did Moses "look ahead to his reward"? How do you believe Moses understood the redemptive plan of God almighty? How is it that we are able to see clearly what Moses was only able to see through the veil of the past? What does this say to you about the sovereignty of God?

Twelve: Jesus and the Tabernacle

And when Jesus had cried out again in a loud voice, he gave up his spirit. At that moment the curtain of the temple was torn in two from top to bottom. The earth shook, the rocks split (Matthew 27:50-51).

In one of my trips to the Middle East, I was sitting one day with an elderly Bedouin man who asked me how I prayed. "Do you pray in the name of Isa?" he asked me. "Isa" is their word for Jesus.

"Yes," I said. "The Bible says that Christians should pray in the name of Isa."

He looked at me and wagged his finger in disapproval and said, "You should not pray in this name. It is haram (meaning shame)." He was saying to me that to pray in the name of Jesus was a degradation of Almighty God.

I looked to my host, a committed believer who lived nearby. I knew that I needed to be careful of what I said next, and I didn't want to get it wrong. It was then that my friend had an inspiration and answered our Bedouin friend.

"If I wanted an appointment with King Abdullah, I would not be able to get in to see him. I have no connections." Abdullah was the king, and his picture was hanging from the goat skin walls of the tent we were sitting in, just above the head of our elderly friend.

"But if I knew Prince Hussain who brought me in to see the king, then it would be no problem!" The elderly Bedouin nodded at the truth in this answer.

"We Christians believe that it is Jesus, the Son of God, who allows us to enter the presence of God. The Bible says we should pray in His name."

As we left the tent of that man, I couldn't help but reflect on the account of the Israelites moving into the land of promise, not far from where we were standing at the moment in southern Jordan in the part of the world that would have been known in ancient times as "Edom." It was in this very land that God gave us a dynamic illustration of the very things we had just talked about under the bright stars sitting in that goat-skin tent.

The Separateness of God

God instructed His people to construct a large tent that would hold His presence. In those elaborate instructions, God made it clear that they were not to come into His presence. It was in very clear terms a visual illustration of the holiness and separateness of God. Not just anyone could walk into God's presence, and that was made clear in the construction of the Holy of Holies and the Ark of the Covenant that were precursors to the building of the temple. It was also a foreshadowing of the coming of Christ.

The biblical account given to us in the book of Exodus tells us that the presence of God hovered over the Israelites in their escape from Egypt as a cloud by day and a pillar of fire by night. As they entered the land of promise, began to establish a new home, and received God's law, it became necessary for them to build a more permanent home for His presence. We find these instructions in Exodus 25:1-31:17. The ESV Study BIble gives us two important keys to the meaning of the tabernacle:

> *First, the tabernacle is seen as a tented palace for Israel's divine king. He is enthroned on the Ark of the Covenant in the innermost Holy of Holies (the Most Holy Place). His royalty is symbolized by the purple of the curtains and his divinity by the blue. The closer that the items are to the Holy of Holies, the more valuable are the metals (bronze→silver→gold) of which they are made. The other symbolic dimension is Eden. The tabernacle, like the garden of Eden, is where God dwells, and various details of the tabernacle suggest it is a mini-Eden. These parallels include the east-facing entrance guarded by cherubim, the gold, the tree of life (lampstand), and the tree of knowledge (the law). Thus God's dwelling in the tabernacle was a step toward the restoration of paradise, which is to be completed in the new heaven and earth (Revelation 21-22).* [27]

It may seem odd to modern sensibilities that Almighty God would manifest Himself in this way to a band of wandering Israelites moving across the desert. But remember that all of these stories are pointing to a greater story that fit into a bigger context. The meta-narrative that is being addressed is that the presence of God is beyond our reach. There are many accounts throughout the Old Testament Scriptures of the terrifying power of God's presence. The tabernacle itself is built in a way that would keep people out and away.

What is the meaning of this? Why would the tabernacle symbolize the Garden of Eden? Why would it symbolize the separateness of God? Why would it symbolize "not getting in"?

The answer is that it carries with it the idea that our sin has cast us out of His presence. Because of our sinful condition, we can no longer be brought in. Sacrifices have to be made, and elaborate cleansings and careful instructions have to be followed just to approach the inner court. All of it is powerfully symbolic of a future event in which the curtain that separates God and His people would be torn in two.

Our Need For Acceptance

This also points to a profound need in the human heart to be "brought in."

As I am writing this, I am on a sabbatical at Cambridge University in England. Everywhere I go in this beautiful city, I am reminded of scholarship, elegance, tradition, and privilege. Cambridge has some thirty colleges, and each have the same basic design of stately middle-age era buildings that surround beautiful garden-lined courtyards on the inside. The campus design is modeled after the medieval monastery of cloisters and inner courts. And like the designed privacy of a monastery, each of these campuses is off-limits to the public. They have gated entrances with porters standing guard to keep everyone out. Entrance can only be gained if you are a student or faculty member of that institution.

The city of Cambridge is a city that understands, as much as any other in the world, what it means to be "brought in." And locked out.

In the community of researchers with which I am staying, there is a young man from an Asian country who recently failed his PhD exams. Since learning of his failure, he has been so devastated and ashamed that he has refused to come out of his apartment. Because of the "shame culture" he has come from, it is difficult for him to face his fellow students.

In a profound way, all of us can relate to what this young PhD student is experiencing. We all know what it is like to be locked out and to feel rejection. In a way, one of our deepest needs is in some way to be "brought in." It is the driving force behind our desire for status, acceptance, and community.

From where does this deep desire for acceptance come?

I suggest that this instinct is at the core of our being. We all know instinctively that we need to be brought in, and the tabernacle/temple is the physical representation of that need.

John 1:14 tells us that the Word became flesh and "dwelt" among us. That word "dwelt" is the exact word that is used in Exodus 33:7. Literally, what the Bible tells us is that Jesus "tabernacled" among us! Jesus spoke of the temple of His body (John 2:19), and Paul taught that because we are in Christ, we are united with Him and "living tabernacles" (2 Corinthians 6:16).

The writer of Hebrews is even more explicit:

> *Since we have a great priest over the house of God, let us draw near with a true heart in full assurance of faith, with our hearts sprinkled clean from an evil conscience and our bodies washed with pure water (Hebrews 10:21-22).*

So you see how the tabernacle in the desert and eventually the temple of the Lord were foreshadowing the coming of Christ? It is only in Christ that our thirst for acceptance is satisfied. It is only in Christ that we are brought in.

There is a remarkable story in John 2 that accentuates this point. Jesus goes to the temple for Passover and doesn't like what He sees. Instead of it being a holy place where people take seriously what it means to come into the presence of God, there is a large market set up for the sale of sacrifices inside the temple court.

Jesus calmly sits down and makes a whip out of cords and systematically clears the market and says, "You've turned this house of prayer into a den of thieves!"

It's the only account in Scripture of Jesus asserting himself in anger. Truly, He is disgusted by what He has seen. When He was confronted later by the authorities over what He has done, He makes this very unusual statement:

> *You destroy this temple. I will raise it again in three days (John 2:19).*

The elders replied, "It's taken forty-six years to build this temple, and you think you will build it in three days?" The Bible then says it wasn't until after the resurrection that the disciples realized what He meant.

The tabernacle and then the temple were built to point to something greater. It is amazing to think of how God would build His grand narrative through the centuries. It was as if He was saying, "You have been kept out of my presence but there is One who will come who will change things! Through Him and only through Him will you be brought in." The writer of Hebrews was particularly locked in on this point:

> *We have been sanctified through the offering of the body of Jesus Christ once for all . . . Christ had offered for all time a single sacrifice for sins . . . By a single offering he has perfected for all time those who are being sanctified (Hebrews 10:10, 12, 14).*

Jesus is the physical demonstration of the presence of God.
Jesus is the Lamb of God who takes away the sins of the world.
Jesus is our "way in."
Jesus is the true and better temple.

Reflect:

Why do you believe it is important for us to see that we are completely unworthy to come into the presence of a Holy God? What does it mean to you that God is perfect in His righteousness, justice, and holiness? What would it be like for us to live in a world in which there was no sense of justice? Why is it important for us to understand God in this way? What does it say of His love and grace that He provided a way in for us?

Thirteen: Our Champion

He will be great and will be called the Son of the Most High. The Lord God will give him the throne of his father David, and he will reign over Jacob's descendants forever; his kingdom will never end (Luke 1:32-33).

As we continue our journey through the Old Testament to find the various passages of Scripture that point us to the Advent of Jesus, it is necessary for me to jump forward from Moses to King David, a period of around 500 years. Of course I want you to know that in that half millennium, there are many examples of imagery that point us to Jesus. Not the least of which is Joshua, whose name in Hebrew is Yeshua (meaning "Yahweh saves" or "Jesus" in Greek), and who God used to bring the Israelites into the Promised Land. As you can imagine, there are a lot of analogies in the conquest of Canaan by Joshua to our salvation in Christ. The picture of Yeshua taking His people into the Promised Land is analogous enough! But for the purposes of this book and our need to be concise, I want us to now turn to the period in Israelite history known as the "Davidic Kingdom."

How David Foreshadows Christ

You may remember that as the people of Israel progressed as a nation, they began to ask God to give them a king. The prophet Samuel was used by God to bring about this new period in Israelite history by the installation of Saul as king of Israel. Saul was not a particularly good king. Just like so many other examples in Israelite history, God was faithful in His promises in His provisions for His people, but then the people messed it up! That is in itself a part of the meta-narrative of God's redemptive work in our lives. It is God's way of painting the picture for us that no matter how hard we try, we cannot bring about our own solutions or salvation. We are totally and completely dependent upon Him.

After the disastrous reign of King Saul, a young shepherd boy named David providentially rose to great fame in Israel and eventually became king.

David was the greatest king of Israel who expanded the borders of the land, and brought about a new kingdom that was blessed by God and feared by the enemies of God's people. He brought great wealth, standing, and security to the people of Israel. He was described as "a man after God's own heart." He was not only a great king, but also a great worshipper who wrote many of the songs that are a part of the book of Psalms.

Although he had many shortcomings and moral failures in his life, he remained faithful to Yahweh. During his reign, the nation of Israel served only the one true God. God used David to instill in His people the idea of a "kingdom," which God would use to bring about His shalom. The word "shalom" means more than just peace, it means God's abundance in all aspects of life.

So you can see how Christ has and will fulfill this idea of a "kingdom without end" that was first introduced by the Davidic kingdom and is built upon in the time of the prophets. There are many examples we can find in Scripture, but let me give you three that I believe are significant:

> *For unto us a child is born, unto us a son is given: and the government shall be upon his shoulder: and his name shall be called Wonderful, Counselor, The mighty God, The everlasting Father, The Prince of Peace. Of the increase of his government and peace there shall be no end, upon the throne of David, and upon his kingdom, to order it, and to establish it with judgment and with justice from henceforth even for ever. The zeal of the LORD of hosts will perform this (Isaiah 9:6-7).*

> *And when he had removed him, he raised up unto them David to be their king; to whom also he gave testimony, and said, I have found David the son of Jesse, a man after mine own heart, which shall fulfil all my will. Of this man's seed hath God according to his promise raised unto Israel a Saviour, Jesus (Acts 13:22-23).*

> *I Jesus have sent mine angel to testify unto you these things in the churches. I am the root and the offspring of David, and the bright and morning star (Revelation 22:16).*

David and Goliath

In addition to David introducing the concept of the kingdom of God, we see the foreshadowing of Christ in many other examples of David's life. Perhaps none are more poignant than the story of David's famous battle with Goliath when he was just a young boy. Maybe you have never thought about how that event prefigures Christ. Here are three parallels that are quite profound:

First of all, David was anointed for his task.

It is significant that David was anointed as king even before he became king. The emphasis on his anointing is important. The word "Christ" or "Christos" in Greek means David was anointed for his task ahead. In a similarly profound way, Jesus was anointed by God Himself at His baptism for the task before Him after staying in the wilderness for forty days and nights.

Second, David was a good shepherd.

David's life pre-figured Christ in that he was a humble shepherd. But more than that, David was a good shepherd, meaning he protected his sheep, cared for them, and was attentive to them. His good work as a shepherd no doubt prepared him for leadership as king. David's understanding of the heart of a shepherd has been immortalized in the 23rd Psalm:

The Lord is my Shepherd,
I shall not want,
He makes me lie down in green pastures,
He leads me beside still waters,
He restores my soul,
He leads me in the paths of righteousness for His names sake
Though I walk in the valley of the shadow of death,
I will fear no evil,
Thy rod and thy staff, they comfort me,
Thou prepares a table before me in the midst of my enemies,
Surely goodness and mercy will follow me all the days of my life,
And I will dwell in the house of the Lord forever.

Only a shepherd would have the ability to write those words! Jesus developed this point extensively in John 11. It's hard not to think of David as you read it:

I am the good shepherd. The good shepherd lays down his life for the sheep. The hired hand is not the shepherd and does not own the sheep. So when he sees the wolf coming, he abandons the sheep and runs away. Then the wolf attacks the flock and scatters it. The man runs away because he is a hired hand and cares nothing for the sheep. I am the good shepherd; I know my sheep and my sheep know me— just as the Father knows me and I know the Father—and I lay down my life for the sheep (John 11:10-15).

Third, David was Israel's champion, standing in the way of all that stood against her.

The epic of David begins when, as a young man, he comes upon an Israelite standoff with the hated enemy of Israel, the Philistines. The fearsome champion of Philistia, the giant Goliath had come out to challenge Israel and to lash insults at her army. David quickly sizes him up, and in youthful exuberance, volunteers for the duel.

At the behest of his older brothers, David prepares for the battle. He refused the king's armor, as he did not consider it as something he needed (see Philippians 2:6), but humbled himself and faced the giant with nothing but a sling. No doubt, in David's mind, the cumbersome giant was not as limber as many large animals of prey he had put down while protecting his sheep.

Most people tend to focus on the courage of David, which was significant, of course. But the more important point is that David became Israel's champion when he won the battle and cut off the head of Goliath. Interestingly, the name "Goliath" is akin to the word "snake," which alludes to another important prophecy about the Anointed One. The very first prophecy in Scripture is Genesis 3:15, that the future Messiah would crush the head of the snake (see Genesis 3:15 and Revelation 20:1-3).

The concept of a champion is important here. Easton's Bible Dictionary defines a champion as "the one between the two." He is the one who stands before God's people and their enemy. I like the New Living Translation of Hebrews 12:2:

> *We do this by keeping our eyes on Jesus, the champion who initiates and perfects our faith. Because of the joy awaiting him, he endured the cross, disregarding its shame. Now he is seated in the place of honor beside God's throne.*

The great English pastor, Charles Spurgeon, once preached a sermon on David as a type of Christ. In it he strongly develops this point that like David, Christ is our champion:

> *The passion of a warrior kindled in his breast at the sound of that profane voice of the uncircumcised Philistine, who could trifle with the honor of Jehovah, the God of heaven and of earth! A further motive was present to stimulate his patriotic ambition. How could David's bosom fail to glow with strong emotion when he was told that the man who should vanquish and slay that Philistine should be married to the king's daughter? Such a prize might well quicken his ardor. But with all these motives acting upon him, his determination to go forth and do battle with the champion of Philistia was prompt and resolute. Now in all this he plainly foreshadowed our Lord Jesus Christ. He loved his own: he was always ready to lay down his life for the sheep. But he loved his Father: "Wist ye not," he had said of old, "that I must be about my Father's business?" "The zeal of thine house hath eaten me up." And then there was the joy that was set before him that he should have the Church for his spouse; that at the peril, not to say the price of his life, he should obtain her; that he should see of the travail of his soul in her, and should be satisfied.*

She was to be lifted up to his royalties, and to share his crown and throne. The new Jerusalem, the mother of us all, was to be unto Jesus the gift of God as his reward; and this inspired him, so he went forth and entered upon the battle for our sakes.[28]

Jesus is the true and better Shepherd.
He is the true and better Champion.
He is the true and better King.
He is the true and better David.

Reflect:

The concept of a champion is one that figures heavily in the story of David. Why is this important in our understanding of what Christ has done for us? How does the kingdom established by David point us to the kingdom established by Christ? Why is it important to see Jesus as our Champion and King?

PART THREE
Promise

Gustave Doré - "The Dove Sent Forth from the Ark"

Fourteen: The Importance of a Promise Kept

For all the promises of God find their Yes in him. That is why it is through him that we utter our Amen to God for his glory (2 Corinthians 1:20).

On March 11, 1942, as the Pacific War raged in the months after Pearl Harbor, the Philippine Islands were invaded by the Japanese. Faced with overwhelming enemy resources, U.S. General Douglas MacArthur was ordered by the Joint Chiefs of Staff to leave his adopted home of Corregidor Island and transfer his base of operations to Australia.

It was a heart-wrenching journey for MacArthur, as he knew he was leaving behind hundreds of thousands of vulnerable Philippine citizens and 90,000 American troops to an uncertain fate. When he arrived at the U.S. army base in Australia, a loud speaker was hastily set up for the tall, imposing American general to address his troops and the world. It was here that he first spoke the words that would later be immortalized in American folklore and in the famous Fallen Soldier statues on the Philippine Islands. He said with his patented authoritative voice:

I have left the Philippines, but I shall return!

It wasn't long before all of the Philippine Islands fell into the hands of the Japanese, and 70,000 American troops were captured, most of whom suffered mightily at the hands of their captors, including over 6,000 who were tortured and killed.

For two long years, MacArthur would repeat those words. He campaigned for the Philippine cause not only with the Joint Chiefs and the administration, but also with the American people. The American press began to publish emotionally-charged stories of the atrocities of Japanese imprisonment on the Islands, including the horrific "Batan Death March" which resulted in 60,000 Philippine and Americans dead. Finally the Pacific War began to turn as the American forces gained an upper hand at Guadalcanal and the Solomon Islands, and MacArthur received the go-ahead for his long awaited plan to invade the islands and recapture his former home base.

On October 20, 1944, after successful U.S. campaigns in the initial invasion, MacArthur waded ashore the Island of Leyte in the Philippines and announced in a nationwide radio broadcast:

> *I have returned. By the grace of Almighty God our forces stand again on Philippine soil—soil consecrated in the blood of our two peoples. We have come, dedicated and committed, to the task of destroying every vestige of enemy control over your daily lives, and of restoring, upon a foundation of indestructible strength, the liberties of your people.*

As they say, the rest of the story is history. MacArthur and the American forces did indeed liberate the Philippines, and the war was won.

The reason this story looms so large in American history is that it captures a very important value. The value of a "promise kept." We all have great admiration for a man who stands in front of the world and makes a promise, and then focuses all his passion on keeping that promise.

This brings me to the next important topic I want us to focus on as we continue our journey to discover the many ways the Old Testament points us to the Advent of Christ. The Lord God made a very important promise to His people. The promise was not unlike the promise MacArthur made to the Filipino people on that fateful day. The promise was in effect,

A day of liberation is coming!

The biblical story makes clear our desperate condition. The enemy has established temporary control over our lost world. This story line is emphasized over and again throughout the Old Testament text. But within the text there is a divine promise.

It is important to understand the meaning of that promise as we think about the reason that Christ came. Because it is not just significant that many signs and stories point us to His coming, it is also important to understand how His coming fit into the eternal purposes of God. Those purposes were made clear in His promise. That promise is alluded to several times in the biblical text as "covenant."

The Meaning of Covenant

What is a covenant? Before I explain the meaning, let me tell you another story that I think will be helpful.

My mother was a credit union manager when I was in college and always kept a close watch on my bank account. This was before internet banking, so it wasn't so easy to know about your account in real time. There were positives and negatives to this kind of arrangement.

On the plus side, my mom was able to keep money in my account when the balance was alarmingly low. On the negative side, this arrangement gave me a false sense of security in future banking relationships.

Of course my mother wasn't trying to enable bad behavior. She was trying to keep me responsible and was good at communicating to me what she had done.

But I will never forget the time I bounced a check at another bank. I was incensed, angered, even disgusted at the unreasonable and unjust charges that bank inflicted upon my already frugal means! I went straight to the bank and asked to speak to a manager.

The manager was as nice as she could be, making it hard for me to get through my prepared speech. When I finished my rant, she kindly explained to me the "terms of agreement" I had signed when I opened the account.

I had forgotten about that.

In essence, I had signed a contract, and that contract was very clear in black and white and impossible to misinterpret. I had to admit while sitting in her office that I really had no complaint at all. In fact, the charges applied to my account had been spelled out clearly and succinctly right there in my contract.

This is the very thing a contract does—it spells out the exact conditions of a relationship just in case there is ever any confusion. If you feel a condition of that contract has been breached, all you have to do is go back and look at the terms, and the issue is then cleared. A contract says in essence, "You do your part, and I will do my part."

There are several examples in the Old Testament of God entering into a relational agreement with His people in which He clearly spelled out the terms of that relationship. These arrangements are referred to as "covenants."

A contract is similar to a covenant, but it differs in one very important respect. A covenant in Scripture is initiated by God, and therefore, He is the one who establishes the terms. In a biblical covenant, instead of "You do your part, and I will do mine" like a contract, God says, "I will fulfill my part of this covenant even if you do not fulfill yours."

The root word for covenant is a Hebrew word which means "to cut." The very word points to the idea of redemption by blood. It gets its root meaning from treaties that were common in the ancient near-East during biblical times. In these primitive arrangements, a local suzerain king would enter into an agreement with a lesser subject (perhaps a tribal leader or warlord), usually after a battle the king had won over that subject.

The treaty would consist of cutting animals in two and dividing the remains on either side of a path. The conquered subject would pass through the pieces of the animal along the path, as if to say, "If I betray this agreement, may I be cut into pieces like this animal!"

Imagine the bloody scene as subdued and conquered subjects are paraded through butchered cattle, sheep, or goats as they swear their allegiance and loyalty to the suzerain king.

In the violent culture of the ancient near-East, one could be sure that the conquering king was serious about fulfilling that gruesome outcome if necessary. It was a very effective way of pacifying conquered foes. There was no mistaking the explicit visual nature of the covenant agreement. We will see in a future chapter how this particular illustration of a covenant also paints a vivid picture of Christ's redemptive work.

There are a wide range of opinions about the meaning of the various covenants that are written about in the Old Testament. Some argue that there is only one major covenant, and all the others are just reflections of that one. Others see three types of covenants; still others see only two types. I know respected biblical scholars on both sides, and so my purpose is not to argue for one or the other. For the purposes of this book, I only want to deal with the general nature of the meaning of covenant and not get into their many nuances.

I think it is important just to remember that in the Old Testament, the Lord God gave His people a promise. That promise was emphasized repeatedly through the expression of covenants.

A covenant is a bond. It is the acknowledgement of an agreement or relationship. It was a reflection of the promise God made of His coming redemption. Keep in mind, when God established His covenant after the fall of man, it wasn't because His people were so wonderful and deserving. It was quite the opposite! He was saying in effect, "Regardless of your faithfulness, I will love you just because I love you" (Deuteronomy 7:8). It was unconditional and unmerited.

This is the truly compelling thing about the divine covenants. They are the gracious means of a relationship with God for a people who deserve to be removed from His presence forever, by a loving God who has no need whatsoever, in and of Himself, for such a relationship. Therefore, the objective of covenant, so often beautifully demonstrated by God Himself, is that expression of intimate relationship, however undeserved and promise for future redemption: "You will be my people, and I will be your God" (Jeremiah 30:22). All of the covenants in

Scripture reflect that promise.

In the following chapters I want us to see four covenants in particular that point us directly to Christ.

Reflect:

What promise has God made to His people? What does that promise mean to you? How does that promise affect the way we see and understand life?

Fifteen: God's Covenant with Noah

> *By faith Noah, when warned about things not yet seen, in holy fear built an ark to save his family. By his faith he condemned the world and became heir of the righteousness that is in keeping with faith (Hebrews 11:7).*

As we have already seen, the life of Noah is a foreshadowing of the coming of Christ. It was a story that fit into the meta-narrative which points to God's love for us and His future redemptive work. In the biblical account found in Genesis 9, humankind had reached a deplorable state of degradation and rebellion, and the Lord God determined to remove His grace from the earth and to bring about a flood.

The waters pouring out over all the earth was a sign of God turning creation back to the void of chaos. As we learned earlier, it was a form of "de-creation." Noah and his family were spared God's punishment on the ark, and the particulars of that redemptive work pointed to a greater redemption.

When the ark reached land and a new era began, God gave the following covenant to Noah:

> *Then God said to Noah and to his sons with him: "I now establish my covenant with you and with your descendants after you and with every living creature that was with you—the birds, the livestock and all the wild*

animals, all those that came out of the ark with you—every living creature on earth. I establish my covenant with you: Never again will all life be destroyed by the waters of a flood; never again will there be a flood to destroy the earth" (Genesis 8:18-22).

And God said, "This is the sign of the covenant I am making between me and you and every living creature with you, a covenant for all generations to come: I have set my rainbow in the clouds, and it will be the sign of the covenant between me and the earth. Whenever I bring clouds over the earth and the rainbow appears in the clouds, I will remember my covenant between me and you and all living creatures of every kind. Never again will the waters become a flood to destroy all life. Whenever the rainbow appears in the clouds, I will see it and remember the everlasting covenant between God and all living creatures of every kind on the earth" (Genesis 9:8-13).

Imagine the scene as Noah and his family exited the ark. It must have been a horrific site as they witnessed the aftermath of the destruction of the whole Earth. All of creation was wrecked and laid bear. The once green Earth was now a barren wasteland. No more Garden of Eden. Nothing but mud and muck—trees ruined and mountains washed away.

In addition, the surviving family must have had the events that led to the earth's destruction fresh on their minds. They had lived through and survived the complete and terrible degradation of the human condition that had resulted in this destruction. The effects of all they had experienced must have been exceedingly overwhelming and traumatic.

Noah's first act on dry ground was to worship the Lord God and make a sacrifice. He must have felt a keen sense of God's grace in that moment. He must have thought something like this:

> *How terrible is God's wrath and the absence of His grace! But He has chosen me and my family as objects of His mercy!*

It must have been a very sincere time of worship when they finally left the ark. But there also had to be a great deal of sadness as they looked over the once beautiful creation which was now completely destroyed. They would have to start again from scratch.

But who was to say that the cycle of destructive behavior would not also start over again? If it had happened before, why would it not happen again? It would only be natural to think this way, in light of overwhelming destruction around them.

However, this time it was different because Noah was the recipient of a covenant promise. God told him prior to the flood that he would destroy the earth, but that he was making a covenant with him. And Noah knew God's promises were true. He was now looking at the dramatic evidence of that.

Theologians point out that the covenant that was made with Adam was a "covenant of works," in that it was conditioned upon mankind's obedience. But the difference in the covenant with Noah and every subsequent covenant post-fall was that it marked a new era of covenants of grace. God promises Noah that He will graciously spare the earth from future destruction as He establishes a new relationship with His people. He promises a new redemptive future.

Many years ago, PBS journalist Bill Moyer, produced an extensive documentary on the book of Genesis. In one particular episode, he asked the well-known black pastor, Samuel Proctor, about the flood. Proctor said in a matter-of-fact tone:

It's about new beginnings. It's about starting over.

He was right. God told Noah and his family to "be fruitful and multiply," which was in direct reference to God's instructions to Adam and Eve. Noah was given Adam's exact same instructions. It was as if God as the cosmic conductor was saying, "Once more from the top!"

What does this covenant teach us? Three things:

First of all, God is calling for reconciliation with the physical world.

God told Noah to renew a relationship with nature. He said:

I now establish my covenant with you and with your descendants after you and with every living creature that was with you—the birds, the livestock and all the wild animals, all those that came out of the ark with you—every living creature on Earth.

God was instructing Noah to a renewed commitment to the material world. Just as He had instructed Adam to name the animals and subdue them, He is now calling Noah to stewardship over His physical world.

We tend to only think of our Christian commitment as purely spiritual. But consider how God is committed to the physical.

The creation story tells us that when God created, He put His hands in the clay and was personally involved. The word incarnation means "putting on flesh," testifying to God's up-close and personal approach to the material world. Theologians point out that this makes Christianity unique among religions in that it affirms the physical.

As we learned in an earlier chapter, Romans 1 teaches that creation bears witness to the presence of a Creator. When Jesus says that even the rocks will cry out His praise (Luke 19:40), He is affirming the assertion of this covenant that the earth has a voice that is continually proclaiming the glory of God, and we are to join the choir! When we look at the beauty of the earth, we can see that it points to His diverse and creative power.

The world that Noah encountered upon leaving the ark was utterly destroyed but would soon rebound. God is instructing him to join in on that restoration.

Second, God is calling for restoration of justice.

God says to Noah:

> *Whoever sheds human blood,*
> *by humans shall their blood be shed;*
> *for in the image of God*
> *has God made mankind.*

He tells Noah that human life has value and dignity. Every human life, in whatever form it takes, is of value because it was created in God's image. When God restored the earth and established a covenant with Noah, He made it clear that the world He has created and now restored is to be a place of justice for all humanity. Under the terms of this covenant in the restoration of the earth and repopulation of humanity, God is holding mankind accountable for the worth and value of every human being regardless of his or her position, status, gender, race, or economic condition. John Calvin builds this point masterfully in his epic work *Institutes* as he reflects on this covenant of Noah:

> *The Lord commands all men without exception "to do good" (Hebrews 13:16). Yet the great part of them are most unworthy if they be judged by their own merit. But here Scripture helps in the best way when it teaches that we are not to consider that men merit*

of themselves but to look upon the image of God in all men, to which we owe all honor and love. However, it is among members of the household of faith that this same image is more carefully to be noted (Galatians 6:10), insofar as it has been renewed and restored through the Spirit of Christ. Therefore, whatever man you meet who needs your aid, you have no reason to refuse to help him. Say, "He is a stranger," but the Lord has given him a mark that ought to be familiar to you, by virtue of the fact that he forbids you to despise your own flesh (Isaiah 58:7). Say, "He is contemptible and worthless," but the Lord shows him to be one to whom he has deigned to give the beauty of his image.[29]

Third, the covenant is calling for a renewed relationship with God.

The most significant thing this covenant teaches us is that God desires a restored relationship with humanity. The truth of this is seen even in the sign God gives Noah. Have you ever wondered why God would choose a rainbow as a symbol of his covenant promise? There is one very simple and powerful explanation for its significance. The clue is found in its shape. Although a rainbow is actually a circle refracting a sun spectrum through the clouds, from the human standpoint looking at it from ground level, it really appears to be a bow. But why a bow?

We get the answer in Ezekiel who says, "Like the rainbow in the clouds, I have seen your glory" (Ezekiel 1:29). The word "bow" in this passage means "war bow." What could it possibly mean that the rainbow symbolizes God "setting

His war bow in the clouds"? Notice the bow is pointing to the heavens. Ezekiel is making the poignant point that God has disarmed His bow and has pointed it upward. It indicates that God is a God of justice because the bow is set and justice will be realized. But it also indicates that He is a God of love—because the bow of His justice is no longer pointed at humanity, but at His very heart. Charles Spurgeon says this:

> *The rainbow, yet again, is a token that vengeance itself has become on our side. You see, it is an unbroken "bow." He did not snap it across his knee. It is still a bow. Vengeance is there, justice is there; but which way is it pointed? It is turned upward.*[30]

Do you see now how the rainbow, and thus the covenant with Noah, points to the day of redemption when God would take it upon Himself to fully pay the price for the sinful condition of all humanity? God would no longer destroy the physical world. There was no need. Because in the course of redemptive history, the price would be paid by a more true and better Noah.

The long-expected Jesus.

Reflect:

How does God allow the evil desires of mankind to play out to the natural conclusion in the story of the flood? What does it say to us about His grace that God does not allow our evil hearts to bring us to a similar fate? What does the covenant with Noah say about His love and grace? How is this covenant fulfilled in the coming of Jesus?

Sixteen: God's Covenant with Abraham

> *He has raised up a horn of salvation for us*
> *in the house of his servant David*
> *(as he said through his holy prophets of long ago),*
> *salvation from our enemies*
> *and from the hand of all who hate us—*
> *to show mercy to our ancestors*
> *and to remember his holy covenant,*
> *the oath he swore to our father Abraham:*
> *to rescue us from the hand of our enemies,*
> *and to enable us to serve him without fear*
> *in holiness and righteousness before him all our days*
> *(Luke 1:69-73).*

It would be tempting to think that every time God established a new covenant in the Old Testament that He was swapping it out for the older one—kind of like changing cars or switching mobile phone plans. But it is important that we not see the Old Testament covenants in this way. Instead, it is more accurate to say that all of the covenants are pointing us to a bigger promise, and each of the covenants are re-stating and re-emphasizing that promise in a new and different way.

This is the reason Jesus explained to the disciples at the first Lord's Supper that the cup was "a new covenant in my blood" (Luke 22:20). Jesus is telling the disciples that on that day, He is fulfilling the covenant foreshadowed by the prophet Jeremiah who said:

"The days are coming," declares the Lord,
"when I will make a new covenant
with the people of Israel
and with the people of Judah.
It will not be like the covenant
I made with their ancestors
when I took them by the hand
to lead them out of Egypt,
because they broke my covenant,
though I was a husband to them,"
declares the Lord.
"This is the covenant I will make with the people of Israel
after that time," declares the Lord.
"I will put my law in their minds
and write it on their hearts.
I will be their God,
and they will be my people.
No longer will they teach their neighbor,
or say to one another, 'Know the Lord,'
because they will all know me,
from the least of them to the greatest,"
declares the Lord.
"For I will forgive their wickedness
and will remember their sins no more"
(Jeremiah 31:31-34).

In the Greek translation of this text, the word "new" is actually the word "renewed." This means that the covenant that Jesus establishes with His blood is in itself a renewal of the bigger promise that God would bring about His redemption.

This is also true of the covenant the Lord God established with Abraham 400 years after the time of Noah. Remember that God had promised Abraham (Abram) that he would be the father of many nations, and that through his seed, he would be a blessing to the entire world. But Abraham complains to God that He has not yet given him a son. In Genesis 15, we find this dialogue:

> *But Abram said, "Sovereign Lord, how can I know that I will gain possession of it?" So the Lord said to him, "Bring me a heifer, a goat and a ram, each three years old, along with a dove and a young pigeon." Abram brought all these to him, cut them in two and arranged the halves opposite each other; the birds, however, he did not cut in half.*

These instructions would have been very familiar to Abraham. It was a signal to him that God was establishing a formal relationship much like a suzerain king relates to a subject who is coming under his protection. Remember that the agreement is established when the subject walks through the animal pieces and makes a commitment to the king, indicating that if the arrangement is broken, he will be torn to pieces like the animals scattered around him. It's a gruesome visual picture, but effective! Abraham is expecting that God will demand that he walk through the pieces.

But then something remarkable happens as Abraham falls into a deep sleep awaiting God's response. Lying right there by the broken pieces, Abraham sees this vision:

> *When the sun had set and darkness had fallen, a smoking firepot with a blazing torch appeared and passed between the pieces (Genesis 15:17).*

The blazing torch is an image of the presence of God. God Himself has passed through the pieces!

The profound significance of this act is that God is saying to Abraham, "If this covenant I am making with you today is not fulfilled, then I will be the one to pass through the pieces." God was saying to Abraham that the end result of this covenant would be that He Himself would pay the price of its broken terms!

Do you see now how this covenant points us to Jesus?

All through the Old Testament, we see God's people repeatedly breaking the terms of the covenant God had established with them. The covenants through time not only served the purpose of both demonstrating God's faithfulness through the ages, but also demonstrated the frailty of the human condition.

So when the fullness of time had come (Galatians 4:4), God Himself came to the earth in the form of human flesh, lived among men, and died on a cross. He was beaten, dragged through the streets of Jerusalem, stretched and nailed to a cross, stabbed by a Roman spear, and torn apart at the crucifixion event. And in that moment when He cried out on the cross, "It is finished!" the veil was torn into two pieces that was shrouding the Holy of Holies in the Jerusalem temple separating God's people from His presence.

And the Abrahamic covenant was fulfilled.

Reflect:

The covenant with Abraham was a dramatic foreshadowing of the eventual death of Jesus on the cross. In what ways does this covenant demonstrate to us the consequences of our sinful condition? What does it say about God's plan? What does it say to us about His sense of justice and grace?

Seventeen: The Mosaic Covenant

To you and to your descendants I will give all these lands, and I will fulfill the oath which I swore to Abraham your father (Genesis 26:3).

One of the most amazing churches I have ever seen is perched on top of Mount Nebo in the middle of the Negev desert overlooking the Jordan River. The ruins of this church were first discovered in an archaeological dig in 1933. Some of the most beautiful examples of Byzantium mosaic tile can be found in its floor. So immense is the excavation of this beautiful church, that its work is not complete to this day. Each time I have visited it through the years, the size and scope of it has increased. Its prominence and beauty in that area of the world have not gone without notice. Osama bin Laden planned to bomb it in the year 2000 before his scheme was thwarted by the Jordanian government. It is truly a treasure of Christian history.

The church was constructed in the fourth century as a memorial to the supposed burial site of Moses. It was here on top of Nebo that God allowed Moses to see the Promised Land before he died.

One of the most striking things about this church is a giant bronze cross that stands at the highest point on the mountain. If you look closely, you can see that the cross is actually embodied by bronze serpents, signifying Christ's statement, "Like the snake in the wilderness, so the Son of Man will be lifted up!" It is truly an awesome experience to stand there in the middle of that Jordanian desert, look at that giant cross, and make the connection to Moses, the people of Israel, and the Sinai covenant that foreshadowed Christ.

Remember that in the intervening years between the time of Abraham and the time of Moses (about 400 years), the fortunes of the people of Israel rose and fell dramatically. You will recall that Joseph's meteoric rise to power in Egypt opened the way for the descendants of Abraham to find a new home and status on the Egyptian plains. But that was a situation that quickly turned sour. In the face of terrible hardship and slave labor at the hands of Pharaoh just sixty years later, God raised up Moses to intervene on behalf of His people. Through His miraculous work, they were liberated from slavery and moved in mass across the Sinai desert toward the Promised Land.[31]

It was here in the middle of that desert that God established His next covenant. I want us to see how this covenant points us to another important aspect of the over-arching promise of God's redemption. As we have seen repeatedly in our journey to find the many ways the Old Testament points us to the coming of Jesus, God uses a variety of images to help us visualize His redemptive plan. The covenant with Moses adds to that mosaic:

> *On the first day of the third month after the Israelites left Egypt—on that very day—they came to the Desert of*

Sinai. After they set out from Rephidim, they entered the Desert of Sinai, and Israel camped there in the desert in front of the mountain. Then Moses went up to God, and the Lord called to him from the mountain and said, "This is what you are to say to the descendants of Jacob and what you are to tell the people of Israel: 'You yourselves have seen what I did to Egypt, and how I carried you on eagles' wings and brought you to myself. Now if you obey me fully and keep my covenant, then out of all nations you will be my treasured possession. Although the whole earth is mine, you will be for me a kingdom of priests and a holy nation.' These are the words you are to speak to the Israelites" (Exodus 19:1-6).

The Significance of This Covenant

There are three things about this covenant that are very important to understand.

First, this covenant points to salvation by grace.

God did not say to the people of Israel, "If you obey me, then I will save you." Instead, God carried them on eagles' wings out of their slavery. They were saved purely by His grace and not by their own merit. It is essential that we understand the order of things correctly! Christianity is different from every other religion because, in Christianity, we are saved by His miraculous grace and then we obey Him. In every other religion, obedience comes first and then salvation.

Second, the covenant points to our need for obedience.

The next dynamic we find in this covenant is that obedience to God flows out of His miraculous salvation, not the other way around. For the Christian, obedience out of love and joy of our salvation is much more freeing than trying to obey so that God will bless us. The person who obeys only in order to get salvation from God is obeying for selfish motives, and that inevitably leads to bondage. But a person who obeys out of the joy and wonder of what God has already accomplished is demonstrating love and gratitude instead of selfishly angling for better status.

When I was first dating my wife, I wanted to learn as much as I could about her. The more I got to know her, the more I wanted to know her. The deeper I fell in love with her, the more I became a student of her because I wanted to find out what brought her joy.

I will never forget our first date. I was a David Gates fan and popped in a tape by David Gates and Bread (that's right—a cassette tape!) I asked her, "Do you like Bread?"

She looked at me awkwardly and said, "Yes?" She had actually never even heard of David Gates or the group Bread. My question to her sounded a little bit like opening a conversation, "So, do you like mayonnaise?"

It was then that I knew that I needed to be a better student of Teri. When you think about it, every relationship we have has an unspoken covenant. The more you get to know someone and want to strengthen the relationship, the more you understand the terms of their unspoken covenant. Our relationship with God is no different. In the covenant of Sinai and the subsequent Mosaic law, God is saying to His people, "This is how you can love me."

Here is the key point: Obedience is our way of loving God. Just as loving my wife means that I become a student of her whims, likes, and dislikes, and learn how I can bring joy to her heart, I am to become a student of God's Word, and to learn how I can love Him more.

Thirdly, the covenant points to the blessing we will receive.

God says that the result of this obedience is that He will make them a holy nation:

> *You will be for me a kingdom of priests and a holy nation (Exodus 19:6).*

His promise is that this way of living results in a better kind of community than what the world has yet known.

Imagine what it would be like to live together with others in a spiritual community without agendas, without power plays, or exploitation. Imagine living in a place where the people around you cared more for others than they did for themselves. A community where commitments were true, honesty was common, and where people were humble, forgiving, and selfless enough to accept and love others without thought of status, bank accounts, connections, race, culture, or social standing. Imagine a place where people loved their enemies, cared for those in need, and blessed their persecutors.

I've just described the new kind of community that Jesus taught in the Sermon on the Mount that directly parallels this covenant.

I'm also describing Christ's vision for the church.

Think of the similarities between this covenant and the Sermon on the Mount in Matthew 5-7. Moses went to a mountain and received a covenant and a law. Jesus went to a mountain and taught the fulfillment of that covenant and law. Twelve tribes of Israel gathered to hear Moses, and twelve disciples gathered to hear Jesus. God called for the beginning of a new nation under a new covenant, and Jesus called for the beginning of a new community established under the covenant renewed. He said that if the church (the inheritors of the Mosaic covenant) could live this way in community, it would be a city on a hill, a light to the world.

The Order of the Covenant and Our Salvation

But if you only remember one thing about the Mosaic covenant, I would want you to remember the order of the covenant. In this covenant and in our salvation in Christ, the order is always the same:

1. Salvation by grace
2. Obedience
3. Blessing of a new community

This is what God desires for our relationship with Him. He carries us on eagles' wings to salvation in Christ; the outcome of our salvation is loving obedience, resulting in the blessing of community. It is always in that order.

This is what Peter envisioned in 1 Peter 2:

> *As you come to him, the living Stone—rejected by humans but chosen by God and precious to him, you also, like living stones, are being built into a spiritual house to be a holy priesthood, offering spiritual sacrifices acceptable to God through Jesus Christ. For in Scripture it says:*
> *"See, I lay a stone in Zion,*
> *a chosen and precious cornerstone,*
> *and the one who trusts in him*
> *will never be put to shame."*
> *Now to you who believe, this stone is precious. But to those who do not believe,*
> *"The stone the builders rejected*
> *has become the cornerstone,"*
> *and, "A stone that causes people to stumble*
> *and a rock that makes them fall."*
> *They stumble because they disobey the message—which is also what they were destined for.*
> *But you are a chosen people, a royal priesthood, a holy nation, God's special possession, that you may declare*

the praises of him who called you out of darkness into his wonderful light. Once you were not a people, but now you are the people of God; once you had not received mercy, but now you have received mercy.

What a promise this covenant makes! It connects the covenant of Abraham to the exodus event that liberated the nation of Israel. God promised Abraham that He would make him the father of many descendants who would bless the nations. Now Israel is poised to enter the Promised Land and to become the people God had foreseen in that covenant. But now it is time for them to enter into a new and special relationship. The nuances of that relationship would further foreshadow and envision the coming of Jesus.

Jesus and the church are the fulfillment of the Mosaic covenant!

Reflect:

The order of salvation revealed in the covenant with Moses is significant to our understanding of our own salvation. We come to Christ by His grace, which leads to our obedience and is followed by genuine Christian community. How does this process help you in understanding your own experience in Christ? How has your heart been changed? Are you in community? In what ways will you need to grow in these areas?

Eighteen: God's Covenant with David

When your days are fulfilled and you lie down with your fathers, I will raise up your offspring after you, who shall come from your body, and I will establish his kingdom (2 Samuel 7:12 ESV).

We have journeyed quite a distance in our search for Christ in the Old Testament. We have traveled across many centuries and searched many stories, decrees, types, images, and now covenants. Most people go their entire lives without considering the many wondrous ways Christ is envisioned from the beginning of time, or how all of the Bible is a "meta-narrative" of God's redemptive work.

Think about how incredible it is that God would lay out His revelation to us in this way down through the centuries. What beauty there is in His purposes! How amazing the extent to which God would go to show us His love!

As we come now to the covenant of David, think about what these covenants mean to us on a personal level. They should strike our hearts at the very core because it is there in the center of our being that we are most insecure. The human heart always wonders about whether it will find love or acceptance. But here is the evidence in the biblical account. God is pointing to His love for His people through these covenants. John Piper says this:

The reason God's covenants with Noah, Abraham,

Moses, and David ought to increase the joy of our faith is that in all of them the main point is that God exerts all his omnipotence and all his omniscience to do good to his people, and we are that people if we follow Christ in the obedience of faith. The most practical truths any Christian can know are that God is all-powerful, all-wise, and all for you. Nothing will have a more important practical impact on the way you use your money, spend your leisure, pursue your vocation, rear children, deal with conflict, or handle anxiety. Heartfelt confidence that the sovereign God is working everything together for your good out of sheer grace affects every area of your life. [32]

So the covenants we are studying together are not just archaic postulations from a distant past that have no meaning in our lives. They are crucial exhibits of the answer for the deeper longings of the human heart, confirming what is most important to our existence. As we come to this next example in the covenant of David, our connection to Jesus and the story of His glorious Advent in Bethlehem is taking a giant leap forward. After all, that city was called "the City of David," and Jesus was to be called by the prophets, "The Son of David."

In 2 Samuel 7, we find King David at the apex of his influence and power in the world. He has been used of God to establish an earthly kingdom that has brought peace and strength to national Israel. He is far from perfect, and his reign as king has had many ups and downs, but he is described as a man after God's own heart. In all the ways God has blessed him, however, David senses that his leadership of Israel is incomplete. He longs for a temple of the Lord God to be built in Jerusalem. He brings this issue to the prophet Nathan, who will speak to the Lord on David's behalf. It was in this context that God uses Nathan to bring this covenant to David:

> *The Lord declares to you that the Lord himself will establish a house for you: When your days are over and you rest with your ancestors, I will raise up your offspring to succeed you, your own flesh and blood, and I will establish his kingdom. He is the one who will build a house for my Name, and I will establish the throne of his kingdom forever. I will be his father, and he will be my son. When he does wrong, I will punish him with a rod wielded by men, with floggings inflicted by human hands. But my love will never be taken away from him, as I took it away from Saul, whom I removed from before you. Your house and your kingdom will endure forever before me; your throne will be established forever (2 Samuel 7:11-16).*

Before I get into the explanation of this covenant, I need to tell you about the literary technique that is employed in many prophecies in the Old Testament. This covenant does what a lot of prophetic passages do—it takes an extended view of a future event and collapses it down so that the near and distant events are seen together at the same time. In this case, the prophetic revelation of this covenant is actually about Solomon in the near term and about Jesus in the long term.

We can clearly see that the first layers of this covenant's promise are for the son of David, Solomon, who would build the temple in Jerusalem. It is also clear that this covenant extends far beyond the promises of Solomon. Look again at verse 16:

Our house and your kingdom will endure forever before me; your throne will be established forever.

Three different times God uses the word "forever." Whenever God uses that word, we should sit up and pay attention because it means He is working something out in His good purposes that will have an eternal influence. How is it that the "throne of David" will be established for all of eternity?

Of course the answer is that a future son of David, through the line of his step-father Joseph, the long-expected Anointed One and envisioned Seed of Abraham, Jesus of Nazareth, would be born in Bethlehem of Judea. He would fulfill the prophecies, foreshadowings, types, and covenants down through the ages. And He would be a truer and better King than King David. He would establish a Kingdom that would last forever.

When the angel Gabriel appeared to Mary in the Gospel of Luke, he said:

Behold, you will conceive in your womb and bear a son and you shall call his name Jesus. He will be great and will be called the Son of the Most High; and the Lord

God will give to him the throne of his father David, and he will reign over the house of Jacob for ever, and of his kingdom there will be no end (Luke 1:31-33).

Can there be any doubt that the Bible teaches that the promise to David that his descendants would rule forever is fulfilled in Jesus Christ? Is there any doubt that this promise is restating the ultimate promise?

As the Son of David (Romans 1:3) and the Lord of David (Matthew 22:45; Psalm 110:1), Jesus now reigns as King in heaven (1 Corinthians 15:25) over the true house of Israel!

Reflect:

In what way was the covenant of David a continuation of the promise of God to bring salvation to His people? How is this promise answered in Christ? How is the kingdom of Christ a "kingdom without end"? A good definition of kingdom is "wherever the king rules." How is Christ ruling in your life? What would your life look like if Christ ruled every part of it? How does letting Christ rule bring peace and strength to our lives?

Nineteen: The New Covenant

Behold, the days are coming, declares the Lord, when I will make a new covenant with the house of Israel and the house of Judah (Jeremiah 31:31).

The story of Israel from the time of David to the time of Jesus is a pretty sordid and depressing one. After the death of David, his son, Solomon, did indeed build the temple in Jerusalem. But it wasn't long before the various descendent heirs of Solomon made a mess of things, and soon Israel was divided into two kingdoms. As Jesus would later warn, "A house divided against itself cannot stand" (Mark 3:25), and that certainly was true of Judah and Israel. The divided kingdom would eventually succumb to various world powers on its borders, and the era in Israelite history known as the "exilic period" began. It was so named because huge populations of Israelites were carried into exile during this time into foreign lands. As His prophets predicted, the people of God would be scattered, and the temple sacked.

Shortly before the Babylonian Exile, the prophet Jeremiah revealed a new covenant to the people of God. The context of this final Old Testament covenant was the rampant disobedience and disregard of the previous covenants God had established.

Over and over again, God's people failed to obey their covenants. In spite of God's faithfulness and mercies that were renewed and repeated to the Children of Israel through the span of time from Abraham to Malachi, His people seemed wholly incapable of fulfilling their commitments. The time of the covenants had come to a close. The stage had now been set for a new and better covenant—one that would last for all eternity and never be broken.

In God's providential plan, even the failure of God's people was a helpful component of the meta-narrative. The inability to fulfill the obligations God required of them was in itself a powerful object lesson. The message through the ages is that humankind is not capable of its own salvation. Covenant-breaking and the subsequent calamities of Israel and Judah say something very important about our inability to make it work on our own. Left to our own devices, we will take our sinful condition to its natural conclusion of complete and utter destruction. Through the history of failed covenant keeping, God is saying something very important about our deepest need. This is the point that D.A. Carson made in his book, *A Call to Spiritual Reformation*:

> *If God had perceived that our greatest need was economic, he would have sent an economist. If he had perceived that our greatest need was entertainment, he would have sent us a comedian or an artist. If God had perceived that our greatest need was political stability, he would have sent us a politician. If he had perceived that our greatest need was health, he would have sent us a doctor. But he perceived that our greatest need involved our sin, our alienation from*

> *him, our profound rebellion, our death; and he sent us a Savior.*[33]

What each of us needs more than anything else is a Savior. The human heart is desperately wicked and deceitful above all things and no one can truly know it (Jeremiah 17:9). Charles Spurgeon once said:

> *Even my attempts at confession of sin are laced with the sin of pride.*

This is one of the big lessons of the broken covenants. We need God to intervene and do for us what we could not do for ourselves. We needed one who would both renew the covenant, and who could also forever sustain the covenant. We needed one who would make peace with God and go through the pieces of God's judgment. It was in this context that the prophet Jeremiah, inspired by the Holy Spirit and looking down through the ages, wrote these words:

> *Behold, the days are coming, declares the Lord, when I will make a new covenant with the house of Israel and the house of Judah, not like the covenant that I made with their fathers on the day when I took them by the hand to bring them out of the land of Egypt, my covenant that they broke, though I was their husband, declares the Lord. For this is the covenant that I will make with the house of Israel after those days, declares the Lord: I will put my law within them, and I will write it on their hearts. And I will be their God, and they shall be my people. And no longer shall each one teach his neighbor and each his brother, saying, 'Know*

the Lord,' for they shall all know me, from the least of them to the greatest, declares the Lord. For I will forgive their iniquity, and I will remember their sin no more (Jeremiah 31:31-34).

It was this covenant that Jesus recited at the Last Supper. He was saying to his disciples and to us that He is the One who has come to renew the promise. He is the sacrifice without blemish who can sustain the terms of that covenant. He is the one who would take the iniquity of us all onto Himself and would establish the New Covenant in His blood. He is the One who would satisfy the righteous requirements of the law by the shedding of His blood. He is the long-expected and perfect fulfillment of all of the covenants!

Reflect:

Jesus said that the new covenant was fulfilled in His blood. How did the blood of Christ bring about this new covenant? How does the blood of Christ satisfy the covenants? How did He take our place? What do these things mean to your faith?

PART FOUR
Law

Gustave Doré - "Moses Coming Down From Mt. Sinai"

Twenty: The Meaning of the Old Testament Law

For what the law was powerless to do because it was weakened by the flesh, God did by sending his own Son in the likeness of sinful flesh to be a sin offering. And so he condemned sin in the flesh, in order that the righteous requirement of the law might be fully met in us, who do not live according to the flesh but according to the Spirit (Romans 8:3).

Now that we have seen how the many covenants of the Old Testament lead us to Jesus, I want to show you how the Old Testament law also points us to Him. This will seem surprising to some. After all, Christ came to fulfill the law, and so doesn't that mean the Old Testament law is no longer valid?

The answer is yes and no. Christ came to fulfill the law, but that doesn't mean the law is no longer valid. Jesus said it like this:

Do not think that I have come to abolish the Law or the Prophets; I have not come to abolish them but to fulfill them. For truly, I say to you, until heaven and earth pass away, not an iota, not a dot, will pass from the Law until all is accomplished (Matthew 5:17-18).

The confusion comes in our understanding of what it means that Christ fulfilled the law. When the Bible says that Christ fulfilled the law, it means that Christ fulfilled the righteous requirements of the law, and that by paying the price of our sinful condition, we now find our righteousness in Him. This is how Christ accomplishes every "dot and iota" of the law. But remember that the law is God's way of showing us how we can demonstrate our love for Him by our obedience, and it reveals to us the core of our nature. We are not saved by the law, but the law does have a role to play in our lives by pointing the way to a better relationship with God.

Think of the Law as a kind of owner's manual. It is God's way of saying to us, "I'm your Creator, and I made you a certain way. If you follow my directions, then you will learn the way to joy and meaning because this is how I made you to live!"

It is Essential to Know the Purpose of the Law

One of the great marvels of modern invention is the hand-held computer that most people carry around with them called the "smart phone." This device was really unthinkable just a few years ago. To think that hundreds of millions of people in our world are carrying around a personal computer that connects them to the rest of the world via the internet is truly remarkable. I'm old enough to remember life without computers, internet, and televisions that required you to get out of the recliner to change the channel. So it is astounding to me how quickly our world has changed.

But imagine if someone was somehow beamed into our world from the turn of the last century and given a smart phone with no instruction on how to use it or even its purpose. Imagine that this person has never even seen a telephone and only knows the telegraph as a means of communication. With no instruction for its purpose, the smart phone would seem like a bizarre oddity, but of no real use. They would think of it as maybe a strange music box or a thick piece of magic glass. As wonderful of an innovation as the smart phone is, it is of no value if you don't know what it is for or how to use it.

It is the same with God's law.

The value of God's Law is that it gives us insight into the reason for our existence. It shows us our purpose. Without a clear understanding of why our Creator put us on this planet, life can be frustrating and confusing.

Here's the point: Unless you know the actual purpose of something, it really is of no use to you. But not only that, if you don't know its purpose, you will not be able to use it to its full potential.

Knowing Your Purpose Leads to Freedom

Many people have a mistaken idea about freedom. They think of freedom as "doing whatever I want to do whenever I want to do it." But is this really a good definition of freedom? Think of what your life would actually be like if you always did what your selfish, demanding, self-serving, lustful, childish self always wanted. It wouldn't be long before you ruined every relationship you have, lost your job, ostracized your family, and probably ended up in prison, a mental health facility, or worse.

The untimely death of British pop singer Amy Winehouse is a tragic example of this very point. Winehouse was one of the most successful female artists in British history, winning an unprecedented five Grammy awards in one night in 2008, including Best New Artist and Album of the Year. After her double platinum album that same year, she was named "Queen of the Brits" and was widely acclaimed as a role model for British girls. But Amy's life had descended toward self-destruction. With her success, increasing popularity and wealth, it seemed that there was no sense of pleasure, or drug, or addictive behavior she would not pursue. *The Birmingham Mail* reported this:

> *In August 2007, Winehouse was admitted to a London hospital following an overdose. The star was said to have come close to death after taking cocaine, ecstasy, ketamine, and marijuana. The singer pulled out of a string of tour dates, then quit rehab yet again, to the dismay of her parents. In June 2008, Winehouse was taken to the hospital after a fainting episode.* [34]

In July of 2011, Winehouse was found dead in her apartment after literally drinking herself to death. Her bodyguard said she spent the last hours of her life drinking vodka while watching You-Tube videos of her past performances. Ironically, Winehouse's death, at the age of twenty-seven, coincides with a surprising list of other celebrities who died at that exact age, a phenomenon now referred to as "The 27 Club." The list is a kind of "Who's Who" of self-destruction, including Janis Joplin, Jimmi Hendrix, Jim Morrison, Brian Wilson and at least twenty other celebrities. This tragic list of popular and materially successful young people who died way too young serves as a stark reminder of the destructive result of "doing what you want to do whenever you want to do it."

Instead of our common misconception, a good way to understand true freedom is to think of our created purpose. Take the gold fish, for example.[35] If a fish in a fish bowl decided that true freedom means to live outside the bowl and jumped out onto the couch, is the fish more free on the couch than it was in the fish bowl? No. The reason is that fish are created to live in water. The fish is only truly free when it is doing the very thing it was created to do, which is to swim in water.

And the same is true for you and me. We are only truly free when we live our lives according to the purpose for which God has created us. This is what the law accomplishes. It gives us clear directions from our Creator about how we were created to live. And ironically, the more we live according to our purpose, the more truly free we become!

So in this way, the law still has value to us in that it points us to the reason for our existence. But to understand how the law is useful to us in this way, I need to show you the different kinds of laws, how these laws point us to Jesus, and how they are fulfilled in Him.

Reflect

What does it mean to have freedom? What does it mean to live according to His purpose? How does finding our purpose set us free?

Twenty-One: The Types of Old Testament Law

So the law was our guardian until Christ came that we might be justified by faith (Galatians 3:24).

Not all the laws we find in the Old Testament were created equal. Some of them were written for a certain time and place and are no longer particularly relevant. The rest were written for all humanity for all time. Maybe you are wondering why there is a distinction. Why would there need to be various kinds of laws—doesn't that complicate things? From time to time, I hear a critic of Christianity or biblical theism bring up some seemingly remote Old Testament law as proof that the Bible is archaic and primitive and therefore should not be taken seriously.

But these critics are lifting Scriptures out of the original context and building an unfair argument without considering the particular reason that remote law is in the text for that particular time. Some laws were necessary and important in their time, but that time has now passed. So the argument against the Bible because of its historical distinctions is really irrelevant. It would be a little bit like saying, "Look at that silly white wig Thomas Jefferson is wearing. Why in the world would we pay attention to the Declaration of Independence!"

So why are there different kinds of laws if they just confuse people? The answer is that the Bible is an unfolding story that reveals an eternal truth. God works in history. And as time has passed, His unfolding narrative has reached periods of fulfillment in which old things pass away, and new things begin.

Such is the case for the nation of Israel who brought about the messianic seed of redemption. That nation was God's chosen people who were to foreshadow the coming of Christ and the church. God established that nation in ancient times through their father Abraham, showed them how to survive in a time and place in which they were surrounded by idolatrous nations, and had a primitive understanding of their Creator. In that context, various kinds of laws were given to them. They can be classified in three different ways.

First, God gave the Moral Law.

God first gave the moral law to our father Adam and to our mother Eve. Even though our first parents rebelled against God, we still have traces of that moral law written into our consciousness. Paul says this in Romans 2:14-15:

> *For when Gentiles, who do not have the law, by nature do what the law requires, they are a law to themselves, even though they do not have the law. They show that the work of the law is written on their hearts, while their conscience also bears witness, and their conflicting thoughts accuse or even excuse them.*

God also gave a summary of that moral law to Moses on Mount Sinai. Although some of the moral law was written specifically for the nation of Israel, the basic moral principles called the Ten Commandments were to be a moral code for all people at all times.

Second, God gave the Ceremonial Law.

The ceremonial law instructed Israel in its tabernacle and temple worship and was intended for a certain time and place. Christ is the fulfillment of the tabernacle and temple, and these laws are no longer necessary, but there are certain aspects of these laws that are important nonetheless. For instance, the ceremonial law teaches us that our hearts need to be prepared for worship, and that we should take it seriously.

We should keep in mind when learning about the ceremonial laws of ancient Israel that although they no longer apply to our lives, there had to have been a reason that God put them in place in their particular time. It is helpful to know that reason and to reflect on how that can apply to our own situation.

Third, God gave the Civil Law.

In addition to the moral and ceremonial law, God gave the civil law to national Israel. The civil law contained particular precepts and principles that would govern the everyday lives of the ancient Israelites. God gave them these laws to protect them from threats from within and without until the Messiah would come. After Christ came and was rejected by Israel, God lifted His hand of protection from them, and the nation was destroyed by the Romans in 70 A.D. along with the temple. Therefore, the need for the ceremonial and civil laws were subsequently swept away.

But as I said earlier, this does not mean these laws are completely irrelevant. Paul wrote to Timothy in 2 Timothy 2:

> *All Scripture is God-breathed and is useful for teaching, rebuking, correcting and training in righteousness, so that the servant of God may be thoroughly equipped for every good work (2 Timothy 2:16-17).*

So it is useful for us to study these laws and gain an understanding of their underlying principles. Even a law that is no longer culturally relevant has something to say to us about the reason that it was given and how it should be applied to our lives today. David Murray says it this way:

> *The underlying principles of justice in the Civil Law should be studied and applied in appropriate ways to our own day.* [36]

The point is that each of these laws leads us to something bigger and should be seen in a greater context. That leads us to our subject for the next chapter—how the Law is fulfilled in Christ.

Reflect:

Why is it important to know the differences between the various laws? What does the law say about the love of God? What does the law say about our understanding of how to love God?

Twenty-Two: The Fulfillment of the Law

Christ is the culmination of the law so that there may be righteousness for everyone who believes (Romans 10:4).

Throughout my entire life, my dad was my mentor. He pastored for over forty years in Oklahoma City and was a faithful and loving husband, father, and servant of the church. Though he went to be with the Lord in 2013, there are certain things my dad taught that have traveled from my memory, to my heart, and to my very way of thinking. So complete was my dad's influence in my life that when I read certain passages of Scripture, I can hear his explanation as if he was standing right next to me. James 1:23-24 is one of those passages. In it, James makes this statement about the Law:

Anyone who listens to the word but does not do what it says is like someone who looks at his face in a mirror and, after looking at himself, goes away and immediately forgets what he looks like (James 1:23-24).

My dad would say that it is helpful to think of the law as a mirror. It reveals your sin to you, but it cannot remove the sin from you. This has always been an effective key to help me understand the purpose of the law. Think of the law as a reflection of the deepest struggles of your inner self. When you look deeply into these ancient precepts, you can uncover the most significant issues at play in the human heart. What is humankind's biggest problem? Look at the Ten Commandments to find the answer. Our biggest problem is that we idolize and worship the wrong things. Our problem is that we attempt to live our lives outside of God's purpose. Just as a fish is created for water, we were created for worship. And whether we admit it or not, our hearts will inevitably move toward that worship instinct.

The truth is all of us are worshipping something. We were made for it, and if we are not worshipping the Lord God, we will put something else at the center of our hearts. But whatever we put at the center that is not God will end up condemning and destroying us.

Our Biggest Problem

The main issue in our sin, therefore, is idolatry. It was the sin in the garden of our first parents, Adam and Eve, and it is at the core of all of our rebellion against God. In our fallen state, our hearts are seeking to replace God. The result is that we look for life and salvation in other things.

Martin Luther made this point in his writing about the Ten Commandments. In it he proposed that the commands as a whole were focused primarily on the issue of idolatry—that the first commandment was the main focus, and the other commandments were simply manifestations flowing out of that first command. So the reason for stealing, coveting, lying, adultery, etc. is because of our tendency to put other things in the place of God. Our biggest problem, in other words, is in what we worship besides God. Luther says it like this:

> *All those who do not at all times trust God and do not in all their works or sufferings, life and death, trust in His favor, grace and good-will, but seek His favor in other things or in themselves, do not keep this [First] Commandment, and practice real idolatry, even if they were to do the works of all the other Commandments, and in addition had all the prayers, obedience, patience, and chastity of all the saints combined. For the chief work is not present, without which all the others are nothing but mere sham, show and pretense, with nothing back of them…If we doubt or do not believe that God is gracious to us and is pleased with us, or if we presumptuously expect to please Him only through and after our works, then it is all pure deception, outwardly honoring God, but inwardly setting up self as a false [savior]…(Part X. XI).* [37]

Maybe you've never thought of idolatry as being a real problem in our modern age. Maybe you think of idolatry as something that primitive people did as a part of ancient, cultic, worship rites. But let me suggest several ways in which we are just as idolatrous as primitive people bowing down to wooden idols:

1. Some people idolize their wealth and status. Many people measure their sense of self-worth by their net worth. We live in a materialistic age that says,

"Whoever has the most toys wins!" The problem, of course, is that you can't take the toys with you into eternity. My dad used to opine, "Notice you never see a funeral limo pulling a U-Haul trailer." Money might buy temporary happiness, but it can't last. While some measure of happiness and well-being is found in having money, studies have shown that people are not any more happy with fantastic wealth than they are with a moderate income. And people who gain their identity in riches are living on shaky ground. The lesson is that money can bring you some happiness, but it can't bring you ultimate fulfillment.

2. Some people idolize their family. Many parents center their entire lives around their children. If you make your kids the most important thing in your life, there will come a day when they will disappoint you. No child can handle the burden of being an idol. If you don't believe kids can become idols, just watch Little League sporting activities and the worship that goes on in football, soccer, baseball, and softball fields all across America every weekend!

3. Some people idolize their bodies. The beauty and fitness industry in the United States is a multi-billion dollar industry. The fastest growing and most lucrative medical career in the U.S. is plastic surgery.

4. Some people idolize relationships. Idolizing another person is what psychologists call "co-

dependency." If there is someone in your life that has a bigger place in your heart than God, then that relationship will eventually wreck you. Co-dependency says, "I'm not OK if you're not OK." It is the relational trap of basing your entire sense of self-worth and personhood on the way you believe you are perceived by another human being. Many people are caught up in relational idolatry. A manifestation of this idolatry is the need to be liked or perceived in a certain way. The clothing and car industries are just two examples of companies that market their products not for what they are, but for how they bring status. A sense of status is a very profitable market precisely because of how we idolize our relationships.

5. Some people idolize their careers. Closely associated with the need to be needed is the need to feel successful. It is a great temptation to put a sense of worth and purpose in what you do as opposed to finding worth as God's creation. The problem is that a person's career is finite. If your career has become your god, then what happens when your career is gone? This is the problem with putting an idol in the place of God—it can't last, and it won't bring eternal fulfillment.

So as you can see, we are just as idolatrous in the modern age as humanity was in ancient times. This is because that while cultures, times, and ages have changed, the human heart is still dealing with the same sin nature as always.

The first two commands remain as relevant today as ever.

What We Learn About Ourselves From the Law

Understanding the way these dynamics work is beneficial to your spiritual growth. Knowing these things about yourself can be an effective way to resolve frustrating emotions. When you feel depressed, angry, or agitated, it is good to ask yourself what idol is in your life that is causing those emotions. Preachers are not the only ones who preach sermons. Sometimes you need to preach sermons to yourself. When you uncover an unreasonable emotion, sometimes it is important to trace the idolatry that is causing the emotion to its root and remind yourself of these commands.

I remember when my son was in high school, and I once lost control of my emotions at a playoff soccer game by yelling some things at a referee that I shouldn't have (I'm sure you have never struggled with this sort of thing.) I was so disturbed by my behavior that I confessed it to my congregation the next Sunday (a dangerous thing for a pastor to do!) The following week at the Oklahoma state high school soccer semi-final game, the head referee (who I had never met), came up in to the stands before the match, shook my hand, and told me he understood I owed him an apology!

Someone in my church had ratted me out!

Maybe this is why James 3:1 says, "Not many should want to be teachers, because (those) who teach will be judged more strictly." In all honesty, I deserved it.

The point is that the emotions I felt at those soccer games were disproportional to their importance. When I reflected on what was happening to me emotionally, it became obvious that I was idolizing my son. My emotion was the result of an idol at the center of my heart. Wanting what's best for my son is a good thing, but I was amazed at how quickly my heart made that good impulse into an idol. Once I diagnosed the problem, it was easy for me to confess it, confront it, and be rid of it.

The Bible's teaching on idolatry is not that we have sinful desires for bad things, but that we have an "over-desire" for good things. Relationships, money, sex, careers, and social status are all good things. But when they are at the center of our hearts and made obsessions of idolatry and over-desire, they are destructive and harmful.

So the Bible does not teach that idolatry is one sin among many, but that it is at the core of our main problem and the reason for all of our sin. Our problem is that we were made to worship and to love God with all of our hearts, and yet our hearts, in sinfulness, are drawn to worship and love other things. Truly, the law reflects the human condition, and the only one who can fully fulfill the law is Jesus.

When we say that Christ is the fulfillment of the law, we

are saying that the law teaches us how we fall short, and Christ is the solution to that. Like a mirror reflecting the harmful effects of our idolatrous sin, it points us to our need for cleansing. Once we understand the perilous situation we are in, we are able to turn to the only solution for our sin problem, Jesus Christ. So what the law could not do, Christ does. Paul says this:

> *For what the law was powerless to do because it was weakened by the flesh, God did by sending his own Son in the likeness of sinful flesh to be a sin offering. And so he condemned sin in the flesh, in order that the righteous requirement of the law might be fully met in us, who do not live according to the flesh but according to the Spirit (Romans 8:3-4).*

How Christ Fulfilled the Law

So how is it that Christ fulfilled the righteous requirements of the law? The answer is that Jesus lived a perfectly righteous life, perfectly obeyed the law, and was Himself a perfect sacrifice for sin—a "lamb without blemish." So on the cross a great exchange was made. He became what we are so that, in exchange, we could become like Him. Our sin was transferred onto Him on the cross while His righteousness was transferred onto us. John Piper says this:

> *The law was kept perfectly by Christ. And all its penalties against God's sinful people were poured out on Christ.*

Therefore, the law is now manifestly not the path to righteousness, Christ is. The ultimate goal of the law is that we would look to Christ, not law-keeping, for our righteousness.[38]

All that was required of us by the righteous demands of the law has now been answered in the work of Christ. Romans 10:4 says, "Christ is the end of the law of righteousness to all who believe." There are many ways that Christ has fulfilled the needs of the law, but for our purposes I want to name four:

First, the blood sacrifices in the temple were ended because Jesus Christ fulfilled all that they represented.

His sacrifice on the cross ended—once and for all—the need for sacrifice. Imagine what the sacrificial system must have meant to the Jew living during the temple periods. All of life would have centered around the temple where sacrifices were made twenty-four hours a day, seven days a week. The Jerusalem temple was a place attended by hosts of temple priests who would have sacrificed a tremendous array of animals offered by thousands of pilgrims. Blood would have run out the back of the temple in a constant stream. One can only imagine the smell!

Those of us who grew up in Oklahoma City remember well the unique smell of animals being slaughtered. Oklahoma City packing houses were a major employer in our city for over eight decades. At one point, over 20,000 people were working in that industry in a part of town known as "Stockyard City." The Wilson and Company and

Morris and Company slaughter houses in the southwest part of Oklahoma City produced an unforgettable "drift" for the inhabitants in town until closing down in 1988. But as strong and memorable as that smell was, it would have been nothing compared to the constant smell present in ancient Jerusalem. One eyewitness to the festivals in Jerusalem wrote this:

> *Multitudes of people from a multitude of cities flow in an endless stream to the Holy Temple for each festival... from the east and west, from the north and south.*[39]

It seems inevitable to me that thoughtful pilgrims would have said to themselves, "There has to be a better way. There must be a better sacrifice!" It seems to me that the overall effect of the constant presence of blood, mess, and stench as a result of that ancient system would have been to point people to a better sacrifice.

> *John the Baptist announced the coming of that better way when he pointed to Jesus and said, "Behold the Lamb of God who takes away the sins of the world" (John 1:29).*

The writer of Hebrews says this:

> *He entered once for all into the holy places, not by means of the blood of goats and calves but by means of his own blood, thus securing an eternal redemption (Hebrews 9:12).*

Second, because of the new covenant established by His sacrifice, the temple priests who stood in the stead of God's people were no longer needed.

With the establishment of the new covenant in Christ, we are now a royal priesthood in Him, and we reflect the glory of our High Priest Jesus Christ who now has an eternal office.

> *The former priests were many in number, because they were prevented by death from continuing in office, but he holds his priesthood permanently, because he continues forever (Hebrews 7:23-24).*

Third, the physical temple in Jerusalem is no longer a necessary center of worship as Christ Himself has fulfilled the meaning of the temple.

He has paid the ultimate and all-sufficient sacrifice, and in His presence we are invited into the glory of God and no longer need the temple. Jesus made this point to the woman at the well in Samaria in a discussion about the proper location of the temple:

> *Jesus said to her, "Woman, believe me, the hour is coming when neither on this mountain nor in Jerusalem will you worship the Father . . . But the hour is coming, and is now here, when the true worshipers will worship the Father in spirit and truth" (John 4:21-23).*

Fourth, the civil and ceremonial laws have been fulfilled in Christ.

Now that Christ has come and fulfilled the righteous requirements of the law and the covenants have been fulfilled, God's people no longer have the need to find their identity in mere national identities surrounding a temple as in ancient Israel. We are now all sojourners here on our way to a new Jerusalem, and the church has become the new spiritual Israel. (This is not to be taken as a statement about the current political nation of Israel, a nation I support and deeply love.)

So Christ has fulfilled the law in all of its aspects. But how has the law pointed to Him? The law itself has foreshadowed Christ in that it has led us to the righteousness of God; it has demonstrated His goodness, His wisdom, and our need for a Savior.

But perhaps the most important way the law has pointed us to Him is that it leads us to the way of love. James calls this love the "royal law" (James 2:8). In living out the principles and precepts of the law, Christ has shown us how to love God fully. By His great love, He has demonstrated to us what is most important about the law. Jesus made this very point to a young lawyer in Mark 12:

> *One of the teachers of the law came and heard them debating. Noticing that Jesus had given them a good answer, he asked him, "Of all the commandments, which is the most important?"*

Love the Lord your God with all your heart and with all your soul and with all your mind and with all your strength. The second is this: Love your neighbor as yourself. There is no commandment greater than these (Mark 12:29-31).

So you can see that in all these wondrous ways, the law shows us our need for a Savior and leads us to Christ. And Jesus, the lover of our soul, is the perfect embodiment of love to which the law points!

Reflect:

What does the law say about our human condition?
What does the law teach us about our emotions?
How does Christ fulfill the law?

PART FIVE
Prophecy

Gustave Doré - "Ezekiel Prophesying"

Twenty-Three: How the Psalms Point to Jesus

I waited patiently for the Lord;
He inclined to me and heard my cry.
He drew me up from the pit of destruction,
out of the miry bog,
and set my feet upon a rock,
making my steps secure.
He put a new song in my mouth,
a song of praise to our God.
Many will see and fear,
and put their trust in the Lord
(Psalm 40:1-3).

Can you imagine what it must have been like for the disciples when Jesus first appeared to them after the resurrection? They must have wondered if they were seeing things. Perhaps they were relieved to look around the room and see that others were observing the same thing.

Jesus let them touch His hands, side, and even ate with them to prove that He was indeed physically resurrected. It would have been a moment of intense joy and wonder. Their minds had to be reeling at the new reality they were witnessing. They surely wanted to know what all of it meant. How is it that a man they had seen brutally executed a few days earlier was now standing in front of them? It was in this time of uncertainty and wonderment that Jesus said to them:

> *This is what I told you while I was still with you: Everything must be fulfilled that is written about me in the Law of Moses, the Prophets and the Psalms (Luke 24:44).*

So at that highly charged and pivotal moment, Jesus singled out the law, the prophets, and the Psalms as something on which He wanted them to focus. It is interesting that Jesus oriented the disciples to this amazing new reality by recalling to their minds the various Old Testament and Psalmic passages that alluded to a coming Messiah.

I believe the reason Jesus did this was to help them grasp what was happening in the larger perspective of Old Testament redemptive history. It was important that they see it in its greater context. As modern people living in the 21st century, we have the benefit of 2,000 years of Christian history, centuries of theologians, and Bible scholars who have helped us to embrace the intricate meaning of the resurrection. But in those first crucial moments after the resurrection, it had to have been exceedingly difficult to grasp. And in that moment, Jesus went straight to the Psalms.

The Influence of the Psalms on the Apostles

His teaching on the Psalms must have made a lasting impression on them because the New Testament witness written by those same disciples was later packed full of recitations from its pages. His teaching was certainly not lost on them. It was obviously imbedded in their hearts as they taught others how the writers of the Psalms pointed to Christ's coming. In fact, there are 114 different quotes from the Psalms found in the New Testament.

And it is no wonder! When one reads the Psalms, several messianic themes emerge that are obviously alluding to the coming Deliverer. Old Testament scholar, Dr. Derek Kidner, makes the observation that the major themes of the Psalms can be summarized this way:

- God saves by grace, not works.
- God will send a deliverer.
- The Deliverer will reveal God in an unprecedented way.
- The Deliverer will suffer as a sacrifice for sin.
- The Deliverer will reign everywhere and forever. [40]

Does this sound familiar to you? It sounds familiar because it is familiar. The Psalms are best understood from the context of the work of Christ. So the reason the disciples use them so often in the New Testament is because they so succinctly foreshadowed that work. From them we learn He would be both divine (45:6-7) and human

(22:22). He would be betrayed (41:9) and suffer death (22:1-31). But He would rise from the grave (16:10) and ascend into heaven where He serves as our king and priest (110:1-7).

Here is a summary of other important passages that point to Him:

> God's only begotten son (2,110)
> Christ's supreme kingship (2,45,72)
> Role as the suffering servant (28,55,102)
> Healing ministry (107)
> Quelling of the raging sea (65,107)
> Hated without cause (35,109)
> None of his bones broken (34)
> His atoning work (69,72)
> His ascension (24,47)
> That He is judge over the earth (50)

Jesus Knew the Psalms

Perhaps the most powerful example of the use of the Psalms in the New Testament was from Jesus Himself. While He was on the cross, He cried out:

My God, my God, why have you forsaken me!

He was actually quoting Psalm 22. This Psalm is a recounting of the events of the crucifixion. Remarkably, this Old Testament Psalm tells us even more than what any New Testament passage tells us about Jesus. Because it doesn't just recount an event, it actually reveals what He was thinking and feeling:

My God, my God, why have you forsaken me?
Why are you so far from saving me,
so far from my cries of anguish?
My God, I cry out by day, but you do not answer,
by night, but I find no rest.
Yet you are enthroned as the Holy One;
you are the one Israel praises.
In you our ancestors put their trust;
they trusted and you delivered them.
To you they cried out and were saved;
in you they trusted and were not put to shame.
But I am a worm and not a man,
scorned by everyone, despised by the people.
All who see me mock me;
they hurl insults, shaking their heads.
"He trusts in the Lord," they say,
"let the Lord rescue him.
Let him deliver him,
since he delights in him."
Yet you brought me out of the womb;
you made me trust in you, even at my mother's breast.
From birth I was cast on you;
from my mother's womb you have been my God.
Do not be far from me,

for trouble is near
and there is no one to help.
Many bulls surround me;
strong bulls of Bashan encircle me.
Roaring lions that tear their prey
open their mouths wide against me.
I am poured out like water,
and all my bones are out of joint.
My heart has turned to wax;
it has melted within me.
My mouth is dried up like a potsherd,
and my tongue sticks to the roof of my mouth;
you lay me in the dust of death.
Dogs surround me,
a pack of villains encircles me;
they pierce my hands and my feet.
All my bones are on display;
people stare and gloat over me.
They divide my clothes among them
and cast lots for my garment.

The fact that Jesus quoted this Psalm on the cross tells us two very important things:

First, it tells us that Jesus had the Psalms in His heart.

He knew the Scripture so well that it was a natural outpouring of emotion at the end of His life. The Psalms were not just Christ's favorite songs. His spirit was the originator of these things. He knew the Psalms well because He was the author. This fact alone gives us a key insight into the life of Jesus. Church historians point out that the Psalms were a favorite of the early church because they were believed to be the favorite songs of Jesus Himself. The Psalms no doubt spoke to Him at various times and stages of His life. This is a great lesson for all of us!

Second, it tells us of the redemptive purpose.

How incredible to think that hundreds of years before the time of Jesus, the Psalmists looked down through the shroud of history, saw that the Deliverer was coming, and that a divine sacrifice would be made.

A great example of this is found in Psalm 16:

I will praise the Lord, who counsels me;
even at night my heart instructs me.
I keep my eyes always on the Lord.
With him at my right hand, I will not be shaken.
Therefore my heart is glad and my tongue rejoices;
my body also will rest secure,
because you will not abandon me to the realm of the dead,
nor will you let your faithful one see decay.
You make known to me the path of life;
you will fill me with joy in your presence,
with eternal pleasures at your right hand.

The interesting thing about these Psalms of David is that when one reads them from the perspective of Christ on the cross, it takes on a powerful new meaning. In Peter's sermon at Pentecost, he tells us that David actually wrote this Psalm about Jesus:

> *But God raised him from the dead, freeing him from the agony of death, because it was impossible for death to keep its hold on him. David said about him:*
>
> *I saw the Lord always before me.*
> *Because he is at my right hand,*
> *I will not be shaken (Acts 2:24-25).*

But the Psalms are not just meaningful because of how they foreshadow Christ. They are also important for another very powerful and poignant reason—the Psalms lead us to meaningful meditation and Christian worship. They provide a rich template for Christian expression. Theologian and poet, Evelyn Underhill, says this:

> *The Psalms are the gate which admits us to the inner world of Israel's spiritual experience: the world into which Jesus was born, and in which the real preparation of the Gospel was made.* [42]

From early Christian history, the Psalms have resonated with Christian worship because they lead us to sing about Jesus, and they lead us to sing *to* Jesus. When we sing the ancient Psalms, it is as if we are joining the chorus of the ages and agreeing with the eternal choir of His redemptive work. But we are also singing to Him, giving Him praise as our Deliverer and King.

Maybe you didn't realize it, but a significant portion of the great hymns and praise songs that resonate so deeply with Christians around the world comes directly from the Psalms. These songs of worship, written in Israelite antiquity, have a transcendence about them that makes them as relevant from one age to the next. One classic example of this is the famous hymn by Isaac Watts, "Joy to the World!" which was based on Psalm 98. Though it was written in 1718, its effect on us is no doubt as powerful today as it was back then:

Joy to the world! the Lord is come;
Let earth receive her King;
Let every heart prepare him room,
And heaven and nature sing,
And heaven and nature sing,
And heaven, and heaven, and nature sing.

Joy to the world! the Saviour reigns;
Let men their songs employ;
While fields and floods, rocks, hills, and plains
Repeat the sounding joy,
Repeat the sounding joy,
Repeat, repeat the sounding joy.

No more let sins and sorrows grow,
Nor thorns infest the ground;
He comes to make His blessings flow
Far as the curse is found,
Far as the curse is found,
Far as, far as, the curse is found.

He rules the world with truth and grace,
And makes the nations prove
The glories of His righteousness,
And wonders of His love,
And wonders of His love,
And wonders, wonders, of His love!

Reflect

Why do you believe Jesus taught the disciples about the meaning of the Psalms? How does worship help us to understand the meaning of our redemption? Why is it important to worship?

Twenty-Four: How the Prophets Foreshadowed the Coming of Jesus

Surely the Sovereign Lord does nothing
without revealing his plan
to his servants the prophets
(Amos 3:7).

Perhaps you've heard the modern parable about the man who was trapped in a flood and prayed that God would rescue him.

The man heard the voice of the Lord tell him that he would save him; so with this assurance in mind, he sat on his front porch and watched the water rise and waited for the Lord's salvation. Before long, a man in a four-wheel-drive truck drove up and told him to get in.

"No worries," the man shouted to him. "God will save me!"

As the waters rose above the man's porch, a second man in a boat came by and pleaded with the man to get in, but again the man on the porch refused because as he told his earlier rescuer, "God will save me!"

Finally the waters rose above the man's house, and now he was relocated to the roof. A helicopter came by, but with the same predictable result. The man refused to get in because he was waiting for the Lord's salvation.

Of course the man drowned. When he got to heaven, he complained to God that his salvation never came. But the Lord told him, "I sent you a truck, a boat, and a helicopter. You were obviously too stubborn to save!"

I'm sure you've guessed the meaning of the parable. God often works in our lives in ways we don't comprehend, but we are too stubborn or maybe too inattentive to see it. But for our purposes in this book, I want to apply another meaning.

Over the course of our journey to discover the many ways Jesus is predicted and foreshadowed in the pages of the Old Testament, we have seen that God has used different means to deliver His message of a coming salvation. He has used stories, types of Christ, the law, covenants, and Psalms. And as we will learn in this chapter, He used prophecies as well. In fact, when we think about the many ways down through the centuries that God has delivered His message of a coming Redeemer, it almost seems impossible to miss.

But like the man on the porch in the parable, most people miss it.

Back in the third chapter I told you about the mathematician Dr. Peter Stoner. He has calculated the chances of someone randomly fulfilling eight prophecies in the way Jesus fulfilled them, and it worked out to a probability of less than ten with seventeen zeroes. As a reminder of the improbability of that ridiculously large number, I again quote Dr. Stoner's analogy:

> *If you mark one of ten tickets, and place all the tickets in a hat, and thoroughly stir them, and then ask a blindfolded man to draw one, his chance of getting the right ticket is one in ten. Suppose that we take 10^17 silver dollars and lay them on the ground in Texas. They'll cover all of the state two feet deep. Now mark one of these silver dollars and stir the whole mass thoroughly, all over the state. Blindfold a man and tell him that he can travel as far as he wishes, but he must pick up one silver dollar and say that this is the right one.*

In other words, to prove that all of these prophecies came about in history just out of coincidence would be a mathematical impossibility. But now that we have come to the end of our journey, we can see that there were much more than just prophecies that pointed to the coming of Jesus.

But my objective isn't to just show you the overwhelming probabilities or even to convince you to get into the boat. Like the man in the story, it is up to you to make that decision. My purpose is to show you how Jesus was anticipated hundreds of years before the Advent, and the variety of ways that message was delivered. And that objective would not be complete if I didn't show you the many prophecies about the birth of Christ.

But before we look at those prophecies, I need to tell you some things about the Old Testament prophets.

First, Old Testament prophets prepared the way for the coming Messiah.

God installed Moses as His first official prophet to Israel because the Israelites were too terrified to hear directly from God. Although there were many prophets throughout the Old Testament, the Israelites knew there was a greater prophet yet to come. It was Moses who first pointed to that prophet in Deuteronomy 8:15:

> *The Lord your God will raise up for you a prophet like me from among you, from your fellow Israelites. You must listen to Him (Deuteronomy 18:15).*

Second, Old Testament prophets spoke not for themselves, but for God.

The message of the prophet did not come out of his own sense of reasoning, creativity, or bias, but directly from the Lord God. In this sense, the prophet was the mouthpiece of God.

> *I will put my words in his mouth. He will tell them everything I command him (Deuteronomy 18:18).*

Third, the prophetic office was ultimately realized in Christ.

All of the prophets were imperfect. But their inadequacies and imperfections served to remind people that one day a perfect prophet was coming. David Murray makes this observation:

Every deficiency or inadequacy in the Old Testament prophets contrasts with the fullness and perfection of Jesus Christ, the prophet of God. We see that looking back, but the Old Testament believer also saw that looking forward.[41]

As I stated in the third chapter, there were more than fifty different prophecies in the Old Testament that were fulfilled by Jesus in minute detail. But instead of going through each of those prophecies, I want us to concentrate on ten that deal directly with His birth:

1. Jesus would come from the line of Abraham.

Prophesied in Genesis 12:3:

I will bless those who bless you, and him who dishonors you I will curse, and in you all the families of the earth shall be blessed.

Fulfilled in Matthew 1:1:

The book of the genealogy of Jesus Christ, the son of David, the son of Abraham (Matthew 1:1).

2. Jesus would be born of a virgin:

Prophesied in Isaiah 7:14:

Therefore the Lord himself will give you a sign. Behold, the virgin shall conceive and bear a son, and shall call his name Immanuel (Isaiah 7:14).

Prophesied in Matthew 1:18-23:

Now the birth of Jesus Christ took place in this way. When his mother Mary had been betrothed to Joseph, before they came together she was found to be with child from the Holy Spirit. And her husband Joseph, being a just man and unwilling to put her to shame, resolved to divorce her quietly. But as he considered these things, behold, an angel of the Lord appeared to him in a dream, saying, "Joseph, son of David, do not fear to take Mary as your wife, for that which is conceived in her is from the Holy Spirit. She will bear a son, and you shall call his name Jesus, for he will save his people from their sins." All this took place to fulfill what the Lord had spoken by the prophet: Behold, the virgin shall conceive and bear a son, and they shall call his name Immanuel" (Matthew 1:18-23).

3. Jesus will be a descendent of Isaac and Jacob.

Prophesied in Genesis 17:19 and Numbers 24:17:

God said, No, but Sarah your wife shall bear you a son, and you shall call his name Isaac. I will establish my covenant with him as an everlasting covenant for his offspring after him (Genesis 17:19).

I see him, but not now;
I behold him, but not near:
a star shall come out of Jacob,
and a scepter shall rise out of Israel;
it shall crush the forehead of Moab
and break down all the sons of Sheth
(Numbers 24:17).

Fulfilled in Matthew 1:2:

Abraham was the father of Isaac, and Isaac the father of Jacob, and Jacob the father of Judah and his brothers (Matthew 1:2).

4. Jesus was born in Bethlehem:

Prophesied in Micah 5:2:

But you, O Bethlehem Ephrathah,
who are too little to be among the clans of Judah,
from you shall come forth for me
one who is to be ruler in Israel,
whose coming forth is from of old,
from ancient days (Micah 5:2).

Fulfilled in Luke 2:1-7:

In those days Caesar Augustus issued a decree that a census should be taken of the entire Roman world. (This was the first census that took place while Quirinius was governor of Syria.) And everyone went to their own town to register. So Joseph also went up from the town of Nazareth in Galilee to Judea, to Bethlehem the town of David, because he belonged to the house and line of David. He went there to register with Mary, who was pledged to be married to him and was expecting a child. While they were there, the time came for the baby to be born, and she gave birth to her firstborn, a son. She wrapped him in cloths and placed him in a manger, because there was no guest room available for them.

5. Jesus will be called out of Egypt.

Prophesied in Hosea 11:1:

When Israel was a child, I loved him,
and out of Egypt I called my son
(Hosea 11:1).

Fulfilled in Matthew 2:13 15:

Now when they had departed, behold, an angel of the Lord appeared to Joseph in a dream and said, "Rise, take the child and his mother, and flee to Egypt, and remain there until I tell you, for Herod is about to search for the child, to destroy him." And he rose and took the child and his mother by night and departed to Egypt and remained there until the death of Herod. This was to fulfill what the Lord had spoken by the prophet, "Out of Egypt I called my son" (Matthew 2:13-15).

6. Jesus will be a member of the tribe of Judah:

Prophesied in Genesis 49:10:

The scepter shall not depart from Judah,
nor the ruler's staff from between his feet,
until tribute comes to him;
and to him shall be the obedience of the peoples
(Genesis 49:10).

Fulfilled in Luke 3:33:

The son of Amminadab, the son of Admin, the son of Arni, the son of Hezron, the son of Perez, the son of Judah (Luke 3:33).

7. Jesus will enter the temple:

Prophesied in Malachi 3:1:

Behold, I send my messenger, and he will prepare the way before me. And the Lord whom you seek will suddenly come to his temple; and the messenger of the covenant in whom you delight, behold, he is coming, says the Lord of hosts.

Fulfilled in Luke 2:25-27:

Now there was a man in Jerusalem, whose name was Simeon, and this man was righteous and devout, waiting for the consolation of Israel, and the Holy Spirit was upon him. And it had been revealed to him by the Holy Spirit that he would not see death before he had seen the Lord's Christ. And he came in the Spirit into the temple, and when the parents brought in the child Jesus, to do for him according to the custom of the Law, Simeon took him in his arms and praised God, saying:

Sovereign Lord, as you have promised,
you may now dismiss your servant in peace.
For my eyes have seen your salvation,
which you have prepared in the sight of all nations:
a light for revelation to the Gentiles,
and the glory of your people Israel.

8. Jesus will be from the line of King David:

Prophesied in Jeremiah 23:5:

Behold, the days are coming, declares the Lord, when I will raise up for David a righteous Branch, and he shall reign as king and deal wisely, and shall execute justice and righteousness in the land.

Fulfilled in Matthew 1:6:

And Jesse the father of David the king.
And David was the father of Solomon by the wife of Uriah (Matthew 1:6).

9. Jesus' birth will be surrounded by suffering and sorrow:

Prophesied in Jeremiah 31:15:

Thus says the Lord:
A voice is heard in Ramah,
lamentation and bitter weeping.
Rachel is weeping for her children;
she refuses to be comforted for her children,
because they are no more.

Fulfilled in Matthew 2:16:

Then Herod, when he saw that he had been tricked by the wise men, became furious, and he sent and killed all the male children in Bethlehem and in all that region who were two years old or under, according to the time that he had ascertained from the wise men (Matthew 2:16).

10. Jesus will be presented gifts by kings:

Prophesied in Psalm 72:10:

May the kings of Tarshish and of distant shores bring tribute to him. May the kings of Sheba and Seba present him gifts (Psalm 72:10).

Fulfilled in Matthew 2:11:

On coming to the house, they saw the child with his mother Mary, and they bowed down and worshiped him. Then they opened their treasures and presented him with gifts of gold, frankincense and myrrh (Matthew 2:11).

As we can see from this sampling of prophecies and the fulfillment that took place, the birth of the Messiah was foreseen over and over again throughout the course of the Old Testament witness. Individually they may not be that convincing, but taken all together make an impressive list.

He Came at Just the Right Time and Place in History

In addition to all of the fulfilled prophecies, the Bible teaches that Jesus came at just the right time and place in human history (Galatians 4:4). And in fact, His coming in the first century coincided with a startling number of innovations and world political and economic realities that gave unprecedented opportunity for the spreading of the Gospel. For instance, in the first century A.D.:

> The world had its first common language (Greek).

> The world had its first protected road system (Via Romana).

> The world had its first sustainable political situation (Pax Romana).

> The world had its first global economic trade system (Roman Forum).

Consequently, for the first time in human history, people could move about freely and communicate with relative ease, from one end of the known world to the other in relative safety. They could do it utilizing a common language. The Romans were brutal conquerors and overlords, but they were also excellent road builders because they needed a way to transport their massive armies. So in one effect, their rule was opening the world to the Gospel.

Former president of New Orleans Seminary, Landrum Leavell, was a mentor of mine when I was a young pastor. One day we were talking about how to discern the will of God, and he said:

> *The only way I have ever been able to fully discern the will of God in my life was looking back on it.*

That perspective has always been helpful. By looking back, we learn many things about the perfect will of God. When we look back on the circumstances of Christ's birth and see the many prophecies that pointed to His coming, combined with the moment in history in which He was born, we see how the perfect will of God was accomplished.

The "long-expected Jesus" made His appearance at exactly the right time.

That reality became increasingly clear to the followers of Jesus. It is clear that the early disciples were deeply moved by what they found in the Old Testament Scripture concerning Christ. They believed with all of their hearts that Jesus was not only the resurrected Messiah, but also that His coming had been foreseen and expected. Paul the Apostle said this:

> *But God has helped me to this very day; so I stand here and testify to small and great alike. I am saying nothing beyond what the prophets and Moses said would happen—that the Messiah would suffer and, as the first to rise from the dead, would bring the message of light to his own people and to the Gentiles (Acts 26:22-23).*

As we come to the conclusion of our journey, in looking together at the "long-expected Jesus" and all the many ways the message about His coming has been delivered to us, we can say like the disciple Phillip:

> *We have found Him of whom Moses is in the law, and also in the prophets wrote—Jesus of Nazareth—the Son of Joseph! (John 1:45)*

Reflect:

What does it mean to you that so many prophecies were fulfilled in Christ? How does it strengthen your faith? Why is it important for us to understand these fulfillments? What do these things say to us about the validity of Scripture?

Twenty-five: He is Coming Again!

> *Do not let your hearts be troubled. Trust in God; trust also in me. In my Father's house are many rooms; if it were not so, I would have told you. I am going there to prepare a place for you. And if I go and prepare a place for you, I will come back and take you to be with me that you also may be where I am (John 14:1-3).*

Our journey to discover how the Bible leads us to the first Advent of Christ would not be complete without looking at His second Advent as well. Just as the first coming of Christ was prophesied and foreshadowed in multiple ways in the Old Testament, so too, has His second coming been prophesied and foreshadowed. Just as the meta-narrative of all Scripture foresees the redemptive work of Christ in His coming to Earth to offer His life as an atoning sacrifice, so too, does that same narrative say to us that He is coming again for the final culmination of that redemptive work. And just as assuredly as those first prophesies came true in His birth in Bethlehem, so too, will the Bible's testimony of His second coming come true as well. Jesus said this in Matthew 24:

> *At that time the sign of the Son of Man will appear in the sky, and all the nations of the earth will mourn. They will see the Son of Man coming on the clouds of the sky, with power and great glory. And he will send his angels with a loud trumpet call, and they will gather his elect from*

the four winds, from one end of the heavens to the other (Matthew 24:30-31).

A good way for us to end our journey is to be reminded that Jesus is coming again!

One thing I have noticed through the years is that the second coming is a perennial hot topic. If you want to sell books, a good way to do it is to become an "expert" on the coming apocalypse. In my own lifetime, I can think of dozens of books that predicted the end of the world and the coming of Jesus. At times, some of those books have even given the exact date that He is to come again.

I can remember clearly that Jesus was supposed to return in 1982, 1988, 1995, 1999, and a large number of books predicted he would return in 2000. Most recently, books have predicted His coming in 2011 and 2012. I know of one particular man who lives in our city who publishes a book just about every year predicting the second coming—and amazingly, people keep buying them!

But while there is a lot of interest in the details of the second coming, I have noticed that the substantive issues regarding the second coming of Christ are often lost. So as we think about the fact that Jesus is coming again some day in the context of a book that looks at the many ways His first coming was foreseen, I want to make a few points that I think we need to remember about His second Advent.

First of all, the second coming means we should all live expectantly, but not obsessively.

The "long-expected Jesus" is still expected! And we should live our lives with that sense of anticipation. I once saw a man carrying a sign on a crowded downtown street that said, "Jesus is coming again. Look busy!"

The humor in that sign actually alludes to an important truth. The parables that Jesus told that illustrated the second coming all had to do with being ready for His coming. The Bible teaches that we are to live our lives expectantly. But that does not mean we are to live our lives obsessively over His coming. Jesus said, "The day and the hour you know not," which means we cannot know when He is coming, we can only live our lives ready for His return. Living with a sense of anticipation means we carry out the work of Christ while we are waiting. But obsession keeps us distracted from that work. After the ascension of Jesus, the Bible says this in Acts 1:10-11:

> *They were looking intently up into the sky as he was going, when suddenly two men dressed in white stood beside them. "Men of Galilee," they said, "Why do you stand here looking into the sky? This same Jesus, who has been taken from you into heaven, will come back in the same way you have seen him go into heaven."*

Think about this picture. The disciples are looking intently at the clouds, and the angels of the Lord say to quit staring at the clouds and get to work (my own paraphrase). Sometimes I want to say the same thing to people who read more second coming books than read the actual Bible. Jesus told us to "be on the watch," but that does not mean that we should be so obsessed with our watching that we are distracted from the work for which He has called us.

Until the Lord comes again, we have a lot to do on the earth. We should live our lives with a reasonable sense of anticipation about His coming, but it should not be an obsession. People who stare at the clouds tend to not see the work in front of them. People sometimes ask me if I believe we are living in the end times. One thing I can tell you for sure, we are definitely living in the end times! And we have been since the moment Jesus ascended into the clouds. But like the angels said, we shouldn't live our lives staring at the heavens.

Secondly, the second coming says something very profound about our philosophy for the future.

Christianity is a uniquely future-oriented religion. We know the final score, and it ends well. Jesus is coming again to make things right. There will be a new heaven and new Earth, and every bit of suffering, hardship, and injustice will be resolved in eternity. Christianity is a futuristic religion in that all of Scripture, the entire story line, continually leads us to a better day.

Every other religion looks back into the distant past and demands that its followers adhere to the teaching of a founder who is already dead and gone. But not Christianity—our biblical faith says that Jesus is alive and at the right hand of the Father, and one day He is coming again to bring about the culmination of His redemptive plan.

Why is this important? Because you and I will live today according to what we feel about the future. What we think about our future impacts our lives right now.

Years ago, I heard the famous business consultant and motivational speaker, Zig Ziglar, speak about this very thing. He told about watching his beloved Dallas Cowboys play in the NFC playoffs. The game was very close, and the Cowboys even fell behind in the fourth quarter. But Ziglar said he wasn't worried. When the Cowboys lost possession on a key series, he felt no anxiety. As the clock continued to wind down, he was not worried at all. The Cowboys won the game on the last possession when Roger Staubach threw a "Hail Mary" pass to win the game. And the reason Ziglar said he was not worried the whole time was that he was watching a video tape replay, and he had already seen the score.

As Christians, we know the final score, and so we should live encouraged—unfazed by a world of pain, sorrow, and heartache. Paul the Apostle said this in Romans 8:

> *I consider that the sufferings of this present time are not worth comparing with the glory about to be revealed to us. For the creation waits with eager longing for the revealing of the children of God (Romans 8:18-19).*

Third, the second coming means God will finally bring a perfect sense of justice into the world.

One of the most complex issues people wrestle with is the problem of evil and suffering in the world. When I talk to people about Christianity, this is perhaps the biggest objection I hear. The thinking goes like this:

> *God is either an all-powerful God who is in control of the world, and therefore allows evil, or He is a loving God who doesn't want evil, but is powerless to stop it. Evil and suffering in the world mean that God is either all-powerful or all-loving, but not both.*

I think this is perhaps the biggest objection people have to belief in God. They say they can't believe in a God who is either allowing evil, or can do nothing about evil in the world. In their minds, God is either all-powerful or a good and loving God, but not both.

In his book, *The Reason for God*, Tim Keller points out that although this is the question of the ages, we will not get a perfect answer until we get to heaven some day. And that actually, Christianity has the most complete answer to the problem of evil. The answer in Christianity is that, in the end, God will bring about His perfect redemption and justice. Only Christianity says that in the realm of eternity, every tear will be dried and every bit of brokenness will be healed. In fact, the greater our sense of injustice in this life, the greater our sense of joy in its healing in the next. Keller writes this:

A few years ago I had a horrible nightmare in which I dreamed that everyone in my family had died. When I awoke my relief was enormous—but there was much more than relief. My delight in each member of my family was tremendously enriched. I looked at each one and realized how grateful I was for them, how deeply I loved them. Why? My joy had been greatly magnified by the nightmare. My delight upon awaking took the terror up into itself, as it were, so that in the end my love for them was only greater for my having lost them and found them again. This same dynamic is at work when you lose some possession you take for granted. When you find it again (having thought it was gone forever) you cherish and appreciate it in a far deeper way…

Just after the climax of the trilogy, ***The Lord of the Rings****, Sam Gamgee discovers that his friend Gandalf was not dead (as he thought) but alive. He cries, "I thought you were dead! But then I thought I was dead myself! Is everything sad going to come untrue?" The answer of Christianity to that question is yes. Everything sad is going to come untrue, and it will somehow be greater for having once been broken and lost. Embracing the Christian doctrines of the incarnation and Cross bring profound consolation in the face of suffering. The doctrine of the resurrection can instill us with a powerful hope. It promises that we will get the life we most longed for, but it will be an infinitely more glorious world than if there had never been the need for bravery, endurance, sacrifice, or salvation.*[43]

One of my favorite stories I tell quite often (my congregation knows it well) is about a faithful American missionary who retired from the field in Africa early in the last century. The man loaded all of his earthly belongings onto a ship in South Africa and made his last journey from that adopted home he had so faithfully served. It just so happened that the ship he embarked on was also carrying President Teddy Roosevelt, who had just finished one of his famous hunting expeditions in Africa. So when the ship landed in the New York City harbor weeks later, there was great fanfare and huge crowds to welcome the president home.

But there was no one there to meet the missionary. Somehow there was confusion about his time of arrival, and his missionary agency failed to welcome him home. The elderly missionary was therefore forced to somehow make his own arrangements to stay at a local boarding house.

Exhausted, lonely, and despondent, he sat on a bench outside the boarding house and began to pray. Pouted is probably a better word. He complained to the Lord about what he had experienced.

> *I gave my life to you in Africa, Lord. I buried my wife there. I served you faithfully, and yet when I return home a man who goes on a safari gets a better welcome. Is this the way you welcome your servant home?*

One of the maids at that boarding house noticed the elderly man sitting there on that bench and was moved by his pitiful sight. She sat next to him and asked what was bothering him. When the man told her the story and how he had prayed, she had great compassion for him and put her arm around his shoulder and said to him, "Oh mister, don't you understand, you're not home yet!"

There is great wisdom in the comfort that woman gave the retired missionary because it is the reality with which all of us as believers are to live. Our lives are to be seen through that great hope. It is to shape the way we think, live, and serve. The writer of Hebrews says this:

> *For here we do not have an enduring city, but we are looking for the city that is to come. Through Jesus, therefore, let us continually offer to God a sacrifice of praise—the fruit of lips that openly profess his name. And do not forget to do good and to share with others, for with such sacrifices God is pleased (Hebrews 13:15-16).*

The coming restoration means that we live our lives with steadfast hope of a better day. It means that nothing can faze us because we know the final score. Things may get rough, but that is only because we have no enduring city here. We are looking forward to the city that is to come.

And just as the Scriptures so accurately pointed to the first coming of Christ who brought us that hope, they now point us accurately to His second coming as well. And it is with an abiding sense of anticipation that we look forward to our eternal home!

Reflect:

When we are excited about the future, it changes the way we see right now. The anticipation we had for Christmas when we were children illustrates this point. How does our anticipation for things to come change the way we view life? Why is our hope in Christ so important? How does this hope help us to get through difficult times? How will the new realities you've learned in the past several weeks change the way you see your life and your future?

The Long-Expected Jesus Family Bible Study

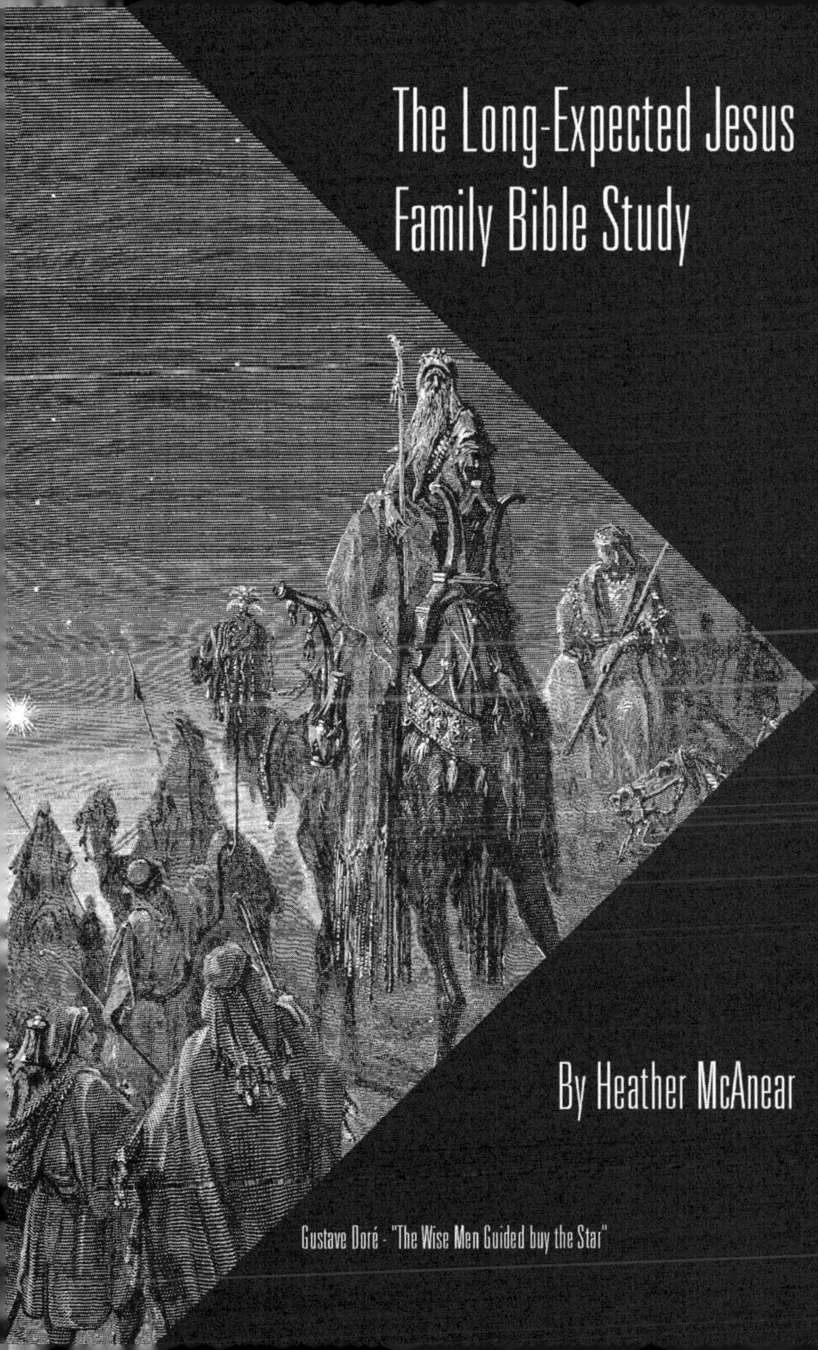

By Heather McAnear

Gustave Doré - "The Wise Men Guided buy the Star"

Introduction

Parents, we are so excited for you to build special memories with your children this Christmas which are centered on God's Word! In order to get the most out of this study, we have some tips for you and a list of all of the supplies you will need for the family activities so that you can be prepared in advance.

First, we will be making simple ornaments on several of the days, so if possible you might want to purchase a small tree for your children to decorate with their Advent ornaments.

Second, the study will work best if you have a chance to read your portion earlier in the day so that you can have time to meditate on and digest your own thoughts before talking through the family study with your children. Plan to spend approximately twenty minutes with your children. Some activities take a little longer, so look ahead. Lastly, pray for your children to be filled with understanding as you participate in this study! They are going to be introduced to some big truths that will shape their faith.

Look over the list of supplies so that you can have them on hand when you need them, and have fun! Merry Christmas!

- Heather McAnear

Supply List:

1. A sonogram from each of your children if you have it; a journal or scrapbook sharing your thoughts during the pregnancy; a photo of an ultrasound, construction paper and scissors
2. Construction paper; cookie cutters (star, circle or Christmas tree), scissors; string, twine or ribbon, crayons
3. Dice or a deck of cards
4. A key of any type (an old key you aren't using or a generic one from the hardware store), twine
5. Paper and pen, your calendar
6. One of your child's storybooks, not too long (for added fun, use a Christmas storybook)
7. Any type of photo of your family or children, even a page from a book would work
8. Popsicle sticks if you are really inventive. Google "free Bible coloring pages" and print a picture of an ark or trace one from a storybook.
9. A stencil or cookie cutter in the shape of a star, twine, string, or ribbon
10. Strips of colorful fabric or different colors of yarn
11. Hot chocolate and marshmallows and/or red grape juice and crackers or bread
12. Blankets and couches to make a tent or an actual tent set up in the backyard (or inside)

13. Small piece of cardboard or heavy paper (you can even use an empty paper towel or unrolled toilet tissue roll), cotton balls, two small sticks from the yard OR Popsicle/chenille sticks, black marker; twine, string or ribbon
14. Be prepared to sing a favorite Christmas carol together. If you are not comfortable singing, use a CD or song played from your phone. *(Examples: Joy to the World, O Come, All Ye Faithful)*
15. Medium-sized Styrofoam balls, colored cotton balls (or colorful gummy candy), glue, ribbon, or twine
16. A piece of red construction paper or red felt, permanent marker, twine or ribbon, scissors, glue, heart-shaped cookie cutter or stencil (optional)
17. Google a picture of a treasure chest to write the true treasures on that God has for us.
18. Today we will talk about our family trees. Be prepared to share with your child their ancestry as far back as possible. Share with him the importance of family heritage and legacy. For the extra activity, use green paper and a Christmas tree cookie cutter, string, ribbon, or twine.
19. Make a gingerbread house using a store-bought kit or instructions you find on Google or Pinterest.
20. Off-white parchment paper, scrapbook paper, or construction paper, sharpie
21. Today's activity consists of talking about family

rules, so be prepared to share with your children the importance of the rules in your home and how much you love them and desire to protect them and point them to Jesus. Additional idea—watch a Christmas movie together. For example, *A Charlie Brown Christmas, The Nativity, Miracle on 34th Street, The 12 Dogs of Christmas*, or *It's a Wonderful Life*.

22. You will need wooded craft sticks, like Popsicle sticks, and twine or ribbon for hanging.
23. You will need candy canes.
24. Go to the Christmas Eve service at your church.
25. Read Luke 2 in your Bible, enjoy your family, and the gift of Jesus!

December 1

Wow! It's almost Christmas! Can you feel the season? Have you seen decorations around town? What are some of your favorite things about Christmas? What are some of your favorite Christmas memories? Dreaming and anticipating are part of what makes the Christmas season so special! This feeling of anticipation is also called "expectancy," like when a woman is expecting a baby! There are a lot of the same feelings and thoughts—and that's probably what Mary and Joseph were going through as they waited for Jesus to be born! And that's exactly what the word Advent means: An arrival that has been awaited. As we read through the Bible together as a family, we hope to make this season of waiting on Christmas day very fun and special.

Family Activity

Show your child his or her sonogram if you have it. Tell him or her about some of the feelings and experiences you had when you were expecting his arrival. Talk about other times of great expectation you have experienced, and ask your child to name some things for which he or she anxiously awaits. To create a visual countdown to Jesus' birthday, use different colored strips of paper, and make a chain by looping one strip through the next and so on. You can hang it from a mantle, the Christmas tree, a doorknob, etc. (any prominent place where you will see it daily). Each day, tear a "link" off the chain and watch it get smaller as Christmas approaches.

December 2

What are some words that come to mind when you hear the name Jesus? Many times when people think of Jesus, they think of only a couple of things: A baby in a manger, a man on a cross, the scene where He fed 5,000 people, the Last Supper with His disciples, or Jesus with children. But Jesus is so much more! Our hope is that over the next month as we study the Bible together, we will all be able to have a larger view of who Jesus is and why He came to Earth as a baby. We are going to spend most of this time reading passages and stories from the Old Testament because many people think that Jesus was only part of the New Testament. We will see that is not the case. From the very beginning of time, Jesus was part of God's plan to save the entire world. In fact, the most popular stories in the Bible point us to Jesus and prepare the way for Him! So get ready to learn a lot, but have fun while we're learning!

Family Activity

Parents ask your children to make a list of words that describe Jesus. After they have shared the words that come to their minds, share your own favorite words that describe Jesus. Next, have them write the words in crayon and use cookie cutters to trace around and cut out paper ornaments to hang on your Christmas tree. Explain why it is so important to have a BIG view of Him. As the Advent season continues, refer back to these words about Jesus and add to them other colorful words to expand your image of the greatness of the Christ-child.

December 3

What is a prophecy? The dictionary defines prophecy as knowledge of the future or prediction under divine inspiration. Many times in the Old Testament, prophets wrote passages about the way Jesus would come into the world, how he would be born, what family He would come from, and about the story of His death. These words were written about Jesus hundreds of years before His actual birth, and it was truly by the divine inspiration of God that the prophets wrote them down. They weren't writing their own words, they were writing God's. The fact that so many prophecies exist, and that every one of them came true is just one way we can know for certain that God is real and that Jesus really did come to Earth to die for the sins of all mankind. As we look at more detailed stories, prophesies, and facts, always remember that you can trust the Bible completely. You can trust God with your whole heart.

Family Activity

Grab a couple of dice or a deck of cards for tonight's Advent activity as you demonstrate the importance and uniqueness of the many fulfilled prophecies of Jesus. Place a handful of the cards face down or hold the dice in your hands. Ask your child to try to guess which card they will draw or what number they will roll. (You can let each child try as many times as he would like.) Talk about how difficult it would be to guess correctly only ONE time, let alone hundreds of times in a row! That is what makes the prophecies of Jesus incredible! They are from God and not random (like card games and dice), and every one of the prophecies came true. Choose one or two examples from today's reading to share with your children.

December 4

Parents, today you'll need a Bible and any type of key. Explain to your children that sometimes the Bible can be overwhelming and even difficult for people to understand, especially the Old Testament. It was written in a very different time in history and even before Jesus was born. Because Jesus wasn't alive when the Old Testament was written, many people, even adults, don't understand how it is connected to the New Testament when Jesus comes to live on earth. (Hold the key while explaining the meaning to your children.) Say something like, "Today I am going to explain to you how Jesus is the key to understanding all of Scripture - the Old and New Testament." We cannot fully understand and experience how a car works without having the key to get inside and start the engine. We also must have a key to enjoy the comfort, protection, and blessing of a warm home. In this same way, we cannot understand any part of Scripture without first understanding Jesus and His message. In the Old Testament, every story and every law was meant to create a longing for something more, a longing for someone who could take away the guilt and shame of sin and some way to be free from the struggles of life, a way to know God. As you grow up, you will learn more and more about God's Word. In the Old Testament, you will see many laws to keep the people safe and pure, along with many miracles to show God's power. You will also see many signs and miracles that point to a Savior who is coming. The New Testament is filled with hope, because people don't have to wait for their Savior any longer—Jesus has come! You have that same hope today, because Jesus is with us still. So this Advent season, when you see this key, let it be a reminder that even when Scripture seems hard to understand, if you take a look at the life and story of Jesus, it can help you understand it better because He is the key to it all. Of course, you can always ask one of us or your teacher at church to help explain anything that you are having trouble understanding.

Family Activity

Use a key you don't need anymore or get a generic key from a hardware store. Tie twine or ribbon through the keyhole and hang it on your Christmas tree.

December 5

There are so many things to love about Christmas! What are some of the things you love? (Let your kids answer, and then share some of your favorite things about Christmas and Advent.) One of my favorite things about this time of year is the anticipation and general feeling of love in the air! As Christians, we know that this is a very special time to set aside our hearts, homes, and resources to celebrate the season of Jesus' birth. But even people who would not call themselves a follower of Jesus are more open to talking about Him during the Christmas season. So as a family, we would like to make the most of this season and ask God to give us opportunities to share the love of Jesus in our conversations and with our actions. We want to watch God open up opportunities, and we are expecting God to use our willing hearts, even children, to shine His light! Don't let anyone look down on you because you are young, but set an example for others in how you live your life (1 Timothy 4:12).

Family Activity

Let's brainstorm some ways we can share the love of Jesus during the Advent season as a family. (Let your kids give you some ideas and then add your own.) Now, let's put these ideas on our calendar, so that we don't forget!

Let's pray as a family that we won't let the opportunities that Christmas brings pass by us. Let's ask the Lord to help us not waste opportunities to share Jesus with others. And let's ask Him to make all of us bold to share about the true reason for Christmas any chance we get! (If you need some help with fun ideas, here are a few: Bake a tasty treat and wrap it up to be delivered to your neighbors with a note letting them know you are praying that they will see and know the hope of Jesus this Christmas. Don't forget to actually pray for them! Take a treat or small gift to elderly friends or family members. Pray with them or let them know you are praying for them. Ask God to show you some widows or orphans who you could visit. Adopt a single mom and help her with groceries, things around the house, or even with providing Christmas gifts for her children. Research how to serve in your community. Call the office at your church—I'm sure they will have ideas or resources. When you serve, pray that God will open conversations about Jesus so that you can share the true meaning of Christmas with those you are serving. As you are out in public and you hear Christmas music playing, you could pray right then that God would use the message of the music to draw someone's heart to Him, and that you would be ready to share with anyone in that place if He were to open the conversation.

December 6

Family Activity

For today's study, we begin with the family activity. Get one of your child's favorite storybooks and read the last page, then the second page, skipping around until you have read the whole story. (Using a Christmas book would be fun!) After reading the mixed-up story, ask your children if the story made sense.

Explain that sometimes when we read the Bible, we focus on the wrong things, and we get the story all wrong, just like this story sounded when we read it out of order. The Bible is not about being "good or bad." The problem with focusing on good or bad behavior is that the focus is off. The hero or villain of the Bible isn't us. The focus of the Bible is Jesus! If we just pick and choose stories and verses randomly, the whole story doesn't make sense. Many people like to skip around, reading this Bible story or that one, like they are not all connected. But it can be confusing and even upset what people think the Bible is teaching. Just like when we read our story book all mixed up, it cannot be understood this way. As you grow up and learn more about God's Word, we want you to understand a couple of big truths. We've already talked about how Jesus is the key to all of Scripture—He's the One they were hoping and waiting for in the Old Testament, and the One who fulfilled all the prophesies in the New Testament. He is the One who clears the confusion and makes sense of the bad things that happen on the Earth so that we can be filled with hope. Today we want you to understand that the Bible is not a bunch of separate stories in a book filled with rules to be obeyed or disobeyed. It's not a book about a bunch of perfect people. Actually, all of the major characters in the Bible teach us their biggest lessons through their mistakes. There is only One perfect person in the Bible, and HE is the hero. The Bible was written to proclaim the story and message of Jesus, our Hero, so that we could have hope here on earth and in heaven someday. The Bible was written as a beautiful love story, better than any Disney tale ever written because this Prince is a perfect Prince, and this Prince came to save the world so that all who believe in Him can live happily ever after.

December 7

In the very beginning, creation was meant for so much more than the beautiful things God made. Romans 1:20 tells us that all of creation points to Jesus. The birth and death of Jesus was planned from the very beginning, not just something God thought up later. God created the heavens and the earth for a specific purpose, and God's plan to send Jesus was in action from the beginning. This is a big concept, but we hope to help you understand more clearly that God was planning how He would rescue you and me from our sin, even before Adam and Eve committed the first sin. Because God knows everything, He knew we would all sin, and that we would need a Redeemer to save us from our sin. He had a rescue plan for us through Jesus. We want you to see the many ways God's creation of the world is like His plan to rescue all of us through Jesus. When God created all things, He gave life to every living thing. When we choose to follow Jesus, He gives us a new life. In creation, God separated light from the darkness, just like Jesus is the Light of the world and saves us from darkness. In the beginning, God produced fruit through the creation of the world. When we follow Jesus, the Holy Spirit produces the fruit of the Spirit (see Galatians 5). These truths will only get easier to understand and grow stronger in your heart as you continue to love God and seek Him throughout your life. We want to show you some ways you can see the story of Jesus in your everyday life! When you see fruit on a tree, it can be a reminder that God has given you love, joy, peace, patience, kindness and goodness to share with the world. When you see light shining in the dark sky, you can be reminded that Jesus is the Light of the world, and He will always overcome darkness. When you see water in a creek, lake or ocean, it can be a reminder that He will wash away all of our sins. When you see a beautiful mountain or a wide open field, remember that His love for you has no end; you can't make Him stop loving you. Go out and experience God's love in the creation that He made!

Family Activity

Have your child hold a photo (any type of picture will work) up to his face, where the photo is actually touching him. Ask if he can see the picture clearly. Now pull the photo away from his face, but cover up part of the photo with your hand, and ask if he can see the full picture very well. Explain that just like we need to have a clear view of this photo with our eyes to be able to see it well, we also need a clear and larger view of creation to understand God's purpose. (You could also make an ornament by putting twine or ribbon on the back of a family photo and hang it on your tree.)

December 8

Today we will look at how the popular story of Noah and the ark points to Jesus. There are three major ways we can see the work and life of Jesus as we think about the ark that Noah and his family floated in during the great flood. First, the name Noah means "rest." In Genesis, we see that part of the consequence for our sin is the work and toil we will do on this earth. Noah's name referred back to God's promise to bring rest through the One (Jesus) who would take away all of our sins and give us rest (or deliverance) from the curse of sin. Secondly, the ark itself is also a symbol of what God has done through Jesus. The people inside the ark were saved from the flood and kept dry, just like everyone who trusts in Jesus as their Savior will be brought safely to God in heaven one day. We are washed of our sins and don't have to face judgment because Jesus already did that for us. Lastly, there was only one door on the ark, only one way in. If someone wanted to be safe from the flood, this door was the only hope. Just like the door to the ark, the Bible tells us that there is only one way we can be saved from our sin, and that is by trusting in Jesus alone (John 10:9; John 14:6). As we are in the Advent season, anticipating the birth of Jesus, we want you to see that the picture of Christ is much bigger than you may have ever imagined. When you look at a nativity with the baby Jesus lying in the manger, it might possibly make you think about Noah and his family floating in an ark made of wood. When you see a picture or hear a Christmas carol, remember that the baby Jesus would grow up to be a man who would save all who trust in Him from their sin.

Family Activity

Print a picture of an ark off of a free coloring page website, or draw or make an ark out of construction paper. If you are really inventive, try building a miniature ark from wood or Popsicle sticks! Ask your children to explain the ways the ark points us to Jesus and continue to remind them of these truths in the coming weeks and months.

December 9

Do you know the song, "Father Abraham"? Today we are going to talk about his story, and how Abraham is connected to the Advert season. (Sing the song with your children or at least read to them these lines, "Father Abraham has many sons. Many sons has father Abraham. I am one of them and so are you. So let's all praise the Lord.") The most difficult and famous moment in Abraham's entire life happened on a mountain, standing next to an altar. Abraham climbed the mountain to make a sacrifice, but he didn't have a lamb with him. He had his son, Isaac. As a child, you need to understand that the love your parents have for you is greater than anyone on this earth—only God loves you more. And God wanted us to understand something very important in this story. God appeared to Abraham and asked him to sacrifice his own son. Abraham did not know how the story would end, he did not know what God was doing, but he trusted God with his whole heart. He knew that God was good, and that if God was asking him to do something incredibly hard, He had a bigger reason (a bigger picture like we talked about previously in our study). So Abraham did what was surely the most difficult thing in his entire life; he climbed the mountain with wood to build a fire with his son as the sacrifice. Abraham went all the way with his obedience, and God met him right in that moment. Just as he was about to sacrifice his only son, who he loved so much, God provided a ram to be sacrificed.

Questions to Ask:
As you heard the story of Abraham, does it remind you of any other stories in the Bible? (The story of God willingly sacrificing His only Son, whom He loved so much.) When we see the details of Abraham's story, we see the story of Jesus! Many years before Jesus was born to Joseph and Mary, Isaac was born to Abraham and Sarah. And many years before Jesus climbed the hill carrying his cross to be sacrificed for all of our sins, Abraham climbed another hill to offer Isaac as a sacrifice. God provided for Abraham that day, and his son Isaac got to live! And just like that, God has provided a rescue for each of us from our sin. We get to live free from the burden, free from the fear of death, and with the hope of heaven!

Family Activity

Using a stencil or cookie cutter, make a star out of yellow construction paper. Put a hole in the top of it, and add some string, twine or ribbon to use it as an ornament for your Christmas tree. When you see this ornament, remember that just as a star shone in the sky to tell the shepherds about the baby Jesus, Scripture tells us that God told Abraham his children would be as many as the stars in the sky! "And I am one of them and so are you! So let's all praise the Lord!"

December 10

When I say the words "coat of many colors," of whom do you think (Joseph)? However, today we aren't going to talk about Joseph's clothes, we are going to talk about all of the many ways his life points us to Jesus. It is truly amazing when we see that God started at the very beginning and has always been using creation and people to point to the saving power of His Son! The most important thing to God is rescuing His people; He doesn't want anyone to miss the point of the story. So He will use anything He can to get our attention and to help us understand the life of Jesus. The life of Joseph is such a wonderful example of this fact. Many years before Jesus lived on the earth, God used events in the life of Joseph to show the people who lived at that time who their Savior was and what he was coming to do. And he uses the life of Joseph for people who lived after him (like us) to look back and see how God was pointing people to Jesus all along. Here are the ways Joseph's life is like Jesus' life: (Parents, use the Scripture references in your daily study to give further detail on any of the points that surprise or are of interest to your children.)

Joseph was a good shepherd; Joseph was loved by his father; Joseph was sent by his father to look for his lost brothers (Jesus came to find and save all who are lost); Joseph was accused of crimes he didn't commit; He was stripped of his clothing; He was sold for silver coins; Joseph forgave those who wronged him; Joseph was both a servant and a king. Those are just a few of the similarities between Joseph and Jesus!

Family Activity

Using strips of colorful fabric or even different colors of yarn, randomly tie the pieces together, creating a rope of different colors. Explain to your children that the colorful rope not only represents the colorful robe Joseph wore, but the way God takes all of the different things we experience in life and ties them together as part of a beautiful story. Both Joseph and Jesus went through very difficult circumstances, but both show that the story is not finished until the final "page." There is beauty and redemption in every story. If you keep waiting and watching, you will see it in yours.

December 11

Today we will talk about how the story of Moses and the Israelites leads us to Jesus. There are many ways the two stories are very much the same, but we will only talk about a couple. First, just like the Israelites were slaves to the Egyptians, we live as slaves to our sin as long as we try to conquer it on our own, without Jesus. Only He can give us freedom, then we will no longer be a slave! Secondly, when the Pharaoh agreed that the people could leave, they had to run out of Egypt very quickly, and their escape was truly a miracle! The Pharaoh changed his mind and sent an army after them, but God opened the Red Sea, making a dry path for all the Israelites to cross quickly to the other side. The moment every Israelite was safe, God allowed the sea to return to its normal state, and the army was swallowed up. In the same way, it was only by a miracle that we were saved. Jesus died on the cross for our sin and came back to life three days later! We are only able to be forgiven of our sins because of His miracle, not anything we could do. A third way we see Jesus in the Israelites' story is in the way God sent Moses to go to the Pharaoh and ask him to let the people go. Just as Moses stood up for the people and fought for their freedom, Jesus stood up to the cross and fought for our freedom from sin and death. Our prayer is that the next time you hear or read the story of Moses and the Israelites, you will remember that this story is only part of an even bigger story!

Family Activity

Option one: Grab a couple of mugs with hot chocolate and a few marshmallows. As you talk about the Israelites, explain the Passover or the Lord's Supper using the marshmallows to represent the unleavened bread and the hot chocolate to represent the wine.

Option two: If you child is older and has accepted Christ, take the Lord's Supper at home as a family! Look at the passage in Matthew 26:26-29 to read the words of Jesus. Use red grape juice and a cracker or even tear off a small piece of bread. Then, feel free to still enjoy a mug of hot cocoa afterward!

December 12

Family Activity

For today's family devotion, make a tent out of blankets and place them over the couches so that you can sit on the floor under your tent. Of course, if you are up for the challenge and you have an actual tent, why not set it up in the backyard and have your family time outside?

Scripture tells us in Exodus that God instructed the Israelites (remember the ones who ran away from Pharaoh and watched as the Red Sea destroyed their enemies) to set up a large tent, and that was where His presence would reside. God made it very clear that He would be protecting them by day and night, but He was not with them the same way He is with us today. As they traveled through the desert on the way to their new home, the presence of God (the tent) would move with them. Once they got to their new land, they built a tabernacle (kind of like a huge church), and that is where the presence of God would be found. In the Old Testament, Jesus had not come to the earth, which means the Holy Spirit had not been sent to live inside of people. Even though all of Scripture is pointing to Jesus, there are certain things that could not happen until Jesus actually came to the earth as a baby, lived a perfect life, and willingly died on the cross for all sins. One of the things that would change after Jesus came to earth is the presence of God. Before Jesus went back to heaven, He told the disciples that He would send a helper who would live inside of them and be with them always. This helper is the Holy Spirit, and He lives in each person who trusts in Jesus and follows Him as Lord. What a relief to know that we don't have to go into a tent or hike to a certain place to be near God—He is with us always! He lives inside of all believers and wants to guide us, comfort us, help us and fill us with His good fruit like love, joy, and peace. The next time you drive by a church or sit in your church on Sunday, remember this story and thank God that He has given you the gift of His presence wherever you are at any time day or night.

December 13

Today we are going to talk about the story of a shepherd boy named David. Have you heard of him? What are some things you know about David? (Some answers could be that he was a shepherd, he fought Goliath, he became a king, a man after God's heart, and he wrote Psalms.) David began as a shepherd boy, who killed the mighty Goliath so that his people would not be mistreated, and his God would not be shamed. Right here we see David pointing to Jesus because Jesus is called our Great Shepherd who cares for us gently and lovingly. Jesus has also defeated sin and death so that we do not have to be slaves to the shame of sin. We can be free as children of God. Eventually David became the king of Israel, who led the people with wisdom and faith in the one true God. David was a great king and during his reign, the people saw what it looked like to live in a peaceful kingdom under a loving king. As Christians, we believe that Jesus is our King who will reign forever, and that His kingdom will be without end. When we think about earthly kings and rulers, we have an opportunity to look forward to our perfect King Jesus and the peace He will bring to the earth when He conquers all evil and sin for all time and reigns in His Kingdom forever.

Family Activity

Cut an oval in a piece of cardboard or heavy paper. Glue cotton balls all over the oval. Glue one cotton ball one-half on the cardboard and one-half off, then draw two small dots in black marker for the eyes. Go outside and find two tiny twigs or use Popsicle or chenille sticks to make four little legs. Glue to the back of the cardboard with them hanging off. Using twine, ribbon, or string, make a loop at the top and hang this ornament on your tree. This will serve as a reminder of David, the shepherd king who paints a picture of Jesus, the Lamb of God, the Good Shepherd and our forever King!

December 14

Today we are going to look at the difference between two very similar words that are, in fact, quite different. What is a contract? The answer is an agreement between two people. Have you heard of the word covenant? Let's talk about these two words. A contract is an agreement signed between two people with what is expected, and what the consequences are if one person does not follow through with whatever it is they have agreed upon. An example of a contract in a family might read like this: "These are the chores for which you are responsible. If you do not take care of your chores, you will not get an allowance (or another named privilege)." Contracts are used in many situations all the time. But this is not the way God deals with His people. God gives us a covenant, which is very different because a covenant basically says, "I will be faithful to my part of the agreement, even if you are not." God made a promise to His people in the Old Testament, and He continued to remind them of it over and over again. We see His reminders in the stories we are studying in this Advent Bible study. God promised to provide a way for all people to know Him, and to save us from sin and death by sending a Redeemer to us. Of course, this Redeemer is Jesus and as promised, God was faithful to every word He said—faithful to His covenant with us. This covenant is the true meaning of Christmas—not just Jesus coming to the earth as a tiny baby, but that He lived a perfect life and fulfilled God's promise by providing a way for us to know God.

Family Activity

Sing your favorite Christmas carol together and talk to your children about the way it points to the covenant of God fulfilled in Jesus. (For example, "Joy to the World" tells of the Lord coming to His people and the need for our hearts to make room for Jesus. "O Come, All Ye Faithful" tells us that our King has come to us and calls us to adore Him.)

December 15

Yesterday we talked about the difference between a contract and a covenant. Today our story is about one of the most famous covenants God ever made! We've already learned about Noah and his family being safe in the ark during the flood. (Do you remember how the ark points us to Jesus?) While they were safe and sound in the ark, rain was pouring down from heaven for forty days! Water covered the earth, and the only people who were saved were the people inside the ark. Why did this happen? Why did God send such a huge rain? Because He was heartbroken about all of the sin and evil in the world. The Bible tells us that Noah was the only person on the earth who did what was right. Can you even imagine how horrible the world would be if every human everywhere was evil all the time? God wanted to give us a second chance and a new start. He wanted Noah and his family to experience grace, and all people after Noah to know how great is His love, but also how serious is sin. Sin will destroy us, and grace will save us. And to make sure every person from that day forward knew about His love, God made a covenant with Noah, "I will never flood the earth again." And as a sign of His covenant (like married people wear a ring as a sign of their covenant with each other), God put a rainbow in the sky. Every single time we see a rainbow, we are to remember that God will never, ever send a flood again. Instead, He sent His only Son, who He loves, to save us from the pain that sin will cause and to give us grace and love. This first promise is an amazing promise indeed!

Family Activity

Glue colored cotton balls (or multi-colored gum drops) onto a Styrofoam ball. The ball should be completely covered and colorful like a rainbow. Use a piece of ribbon or twine to make a loop at the top and hang it from your Christmas tree as a reminder of the redemption found in God's promise of a rainbow.

December 16

We have been talking a lot about God's covenant with His people, and we will look at more covenant stories in the study this week. But as we look at all the ways God showed us His covenant, we want to make sure you understand something very important. God is not making a new deal with His people each time He revealed His covenant of love in a new way. He is re-telling the same covenant in a new and different way, hoping we will understand more and more His love for us, shown in the gift of Jesus. We see repeatedly in Scripture that God's people did not follow the covenant and were not being faithful to God. Through sin and disbelief, by worshipping idols, by turning to earthly kings and giving in to temptation, all people have sinned and followed their own will rather than obeying God. However, God has demonstrated His loving covenant by reminding us of the hope that was to come in the Old Testament and then, finally, sending the Promised One in the New Testament as the baby in a manger, King Jesus!

"But when the time had fully come, God sent his Son" (Galatians 4:4). The Old Testament was a covenant promising things to come, but when Jesus came to the earth, that covenant was fulfilled, and He gave us a new covenant—the promise of His Spirit inside of us. As the Bible says, "This is the covenant I will make with my people. I will put my law in their minds and write it on their hearts. I will be their God and they will be my people" (Jeremiah 31:31-34).

Family Activity

Using red construction paper or felt, cut out a medium-sized heart. Use a stencil for the shape or a heart-shaped cookie cutter. You may also fold a 4"x4" square in half and draw half of a heart shape, starting about one-fourth of the way down on the folded side. Without opening the paper, cut it out, then open it up to a perfect heart shape. In the middle of the heart, either write the reference or entire verse: Galatians 4:4, "When the time had come, God sent His Son!" Tie a piece of twine or ribbon to the backside of the heart and hang it on your Christmas tree to remind you that the new covenant God has made with you is the promise of His Son who came to die for your sins and His Sprit who lives in you—writing His law upon your heart.

December 17

Today we will continue to look at the how God went out of His way to make His covenant clear, as if He was saying, "If you didn't understand what I meant by my covenant with Noah, I will show you again through Abraham. And if you still don't fully grasp how incredibly special my covenant to you is, I will show you through Moses." When we look at God's covenant to His people through the story of Moses, we quickly see three important things that make us focus on Jesus. First, the covenant is all about grace. God will never require us to work harder so that we can earn His love or favor. God has always made it clear that we receive the miracle of His grace because of what He did for us by sending His Son to die in our place. It is not based on what we can do for Him. However, there is a place for our obedience to God, and that is the second thing the covenant shows—that our obedience to God will flow from a heart that loves Him. We do not obey Him in order to make Him love us; He already loves us. We do not obey Him so He will give us forgiveness and favor; He already has given us all that and more. Obedience is one way we show God we love Him, just as a child obeys his parents because He loves them and respects their authority. Lastly, God promises blessing to His people. This is not the kind of blessing that many people think—not like treasure raining down from heaven, or nobody ever getting sick. The blessing God refers to is a better kind of life called a "holy nation." This is the blessing of all people who love Jesus and have chosen to follow Him, living as He instructs in

Scripture: Kind, loving, showing compassion, having joy, sharing the things they have, and forgiving each other. It sounds pretty wonderful, doesn't it? This is God's promise to His people, and this is the third part of the covenant in that very order:

1. Saved by His grace
2. Called to obey God out of love
3. Living the blessing of new and better community

Family Activity

God calls His people His treasured possession, more special than any treasure chest full of money or jewels. Let's put this on paper so we can remember what is important to God and what should be important to us! Google a picture of a treasure chest, color the treasure chest, and write the words to describe the true treasure God has for us (love, joy, peace, community, forgiveness, humble, sharing, care for others, etc.)

December 18

It is very clear to see the connection between David and Jesus when we read the well-known passages that many call "The Christmas Story" telling us about Jesus' birth. First we read that "in the city of David a Savior will be born." But even before we get to the part about Jesus' birth, we see a reference to David that many people don't notice. When the angel visits Mary, we read, "You will be with child and give birth to a son, and you are to give him the name Jesus. He will be great and will be called the Son of the Most High. The Lord God will give him the throne of his father David, and he will reign over the house of Jacob forever; his kingdom will never end" (Luke 31:31-33). Even though Joseph was the earthly father of Jesus, and God was His heavenly father, we see that David was his great, great, great (and so on) grandfather.

Family Activity

Create a family tree of your ancestors as far back as you have dates available. This can be simply listed on paper with lines for each branch of the family or made to look more like a tree by drawing a trunk and some branches and coloring them. Share with your children why heritage and legacy are important. This is all we leave behind! Our possessions and lives will pass away, but the people we impact will impact the next generation, and they impact the next and so on. After making the family tree on paper, use a Christmas tree cookie cutter to trace the outline on green paper. Tie a loop with twine or ribbon and hang it on your Christmas tree as a reminder of the lineage of Jesus and your own family heritage. And most importantly, the fact that you have been adopted into the family of God through Christ!

December 19

As we look at the Old Testament from beginning to end, we see a pattern with the people of Israel and Judah. Over and again, they broke their commitment to follow and serve only the one true God. They repeatedly got impatient and wanted a ruler they could see or an idol they could worship. But God repeatedly disciplined them, forgave them, and loved them. His love never ran out, and He never gave up on them. From the time of Abraham to Malachi, this was God's pattern, as He continued to renew His covenant with Israel. But the time of this covenant had come to an end, and all of the Old Testament set the stage for a new and better covenant that would last forever! The biggest truth we learn from God's covenant with Israel and Judah is that we are unable to obey the law on our own and save ourselves—we need a Rescuer!

"The time is coming," declares the LORD, "when I will make a new covenant with the house of Israel and with the house of Judah" (Jeremiah 31:31). This week we will look at what the new covenant means to us. But for now, let's have a little fun as God's covenant with the house of Israel and the house of Judah comes to a close.

Family Activity

Make a gingerbread house! A fun twist might be to make a gingerbread nativity scene!

December 20

Laws, rules…why do we need them? Have you ever broken a rule? What was the rule, and what happened when you broke it? Have you ever asked yourself, "Why do we need all of these rules anyway?" Or have you ever wanted to live in a house or community without rules? I think if we were all honest, we would admit that at some point, we had the desire to live without any rules or restrictions (yes, even parents have probably had this thought at some point!) However, we see all through the Bible that there is a reason for rules and laws. We really need to understand this completely because this is a big part of understanding what it means to follow Jesus. One of the best ways to understand what laws should mean to a Christian is to look at the example we see in the parent and child relationship. Look at the process of discipline: The child disobeys, the child has natural consequences given by the parents, the child shows repentance, and the parents respond with forgiveness and love. This is the way God has called parents to love their children. Rules are made out of love because they keep a child from harm. If there were no rules, the children would grow up in chaos, not sure what was right or wrong and not sure about the boundaries. The rules point us to the truth; God's Word is the exact same way. The laws God gives point us to the truth and point out the sin in our hearts so that we can know right from wrong. So the next time your parents correct you for a wrong you have committed, remember this is a picture of how God corrects and loves His people.

As a child, you have the opportunity to practice obeying and respecting authority, as you live and abide by the rules in your home. As you grow older, hopefully your heart will be soft, and you will desire to obey and trust God, as you have learned to obey and trust your parents. And, just like God, your parents give you rules to live by because they love you, they want to keep you safe, and they want to give you the best life possible.

Family Activity

Make a scroll of the Ten Commandments by taking a piece of cream-colored paper and wrinkling it. Continue to wrinkle and roll the paper in all directions until it looks very old and worn. Take a brown marker and have your child write out the Ten Commandments on the paper. Engage older children by having them do the writing, and the younger children do the wrinkling. If you want to add an ornament to your tree, tear off a small piece of the paper and go through the same process. You may not actually be able to write all Ten Commandments on this paper. Add twine or ribbon.

December 21

Yesterday we talked about why the law is important to us as Christians. Even though we are saved by God's grace, not by following the law, having a law is important because it identifies what sin is and our need for Jesus. Today, we are going to talk about another important truth about the law. Our hope is that you will grow to understand this truth as you grow to know more about Jesus. God gave different kinds of laws in the Bible, and these types of laws have often confused people.

First, God gave the moral law, which would be the things written in the Ten Commandments. The Moral Law reveals our sin and shows us how to live. Next was the Ceremonial Law, like the different ways they would have to wash their hands, or things they would need to wear. Although this does not apply to our lives today, we can still take a truth from it—like the fact that God wants us to have clean hearts prepared to worship Him, and that we should take our time of worship seriously. Lastly, God gave the Civil Law, which was given to govern and protect the people of Israel. As we look closely at the different types of law given by God to His people over the years, we see the picture of a Father who greatly loves His children, seeking to help and protect them in every aspect of their lives. This is much like the picture of our earthly fathers and the different rules we put into place in our homes, which are given out of love to instruct and protect our families.

Family Activity

Spend a few minutes talking about different rules (laws) in your home and the reason/importance for them. Make sure to take this opportunity to share with your children how much you love them, and why you work so hard to protect them and lead them to Jesus. An additional family activity idea: Christmas is five days away, so celebrate by watching a Christmas movie together as a family.

December 22

So now that we have a good understanding of the purpose of the law (it leads us to Jesus by revealing right from wrong and shows us that we cannot fulfill it on our own), we get to the true meaning of the Advent season, which is Christmas! This far in our study we have seen two very important things revealed through Scripture in many ways:

1. Repeatedly, the Bible is re-affirming the covenant God made with His people from the beginning.
2. God's people have been unfaithful from the beginning and are not able to keep the law by themselves.

As we understand these two things, the best way to sum it up is to look at the law like a mirror. It reveals the sin in our hearts, but cannot remove the sin from our hearts. And this is where our story is so very exciting! God loves us so much that He would never leave us in a situation where we are sure to fail, destined to blow it by not having a solution. From the very beginning of time, He had the very best solution for us. You might remember that a couple of things were needed for the Israelites to make a sacrifice for their sin: A perfect lamb without any blemish and bloodshed. The people would continually be in a state of sinning and sacrificing, but God wanted to give His people a forever solution. He wanted to give us His very own Son, who lived a perfect, blameless life and who is called The Lamb of God who takes away the sins of the earth, so that He could be a sin offering to last for all people who believe in Him. He allowed Jesus to bleed and die on the cross, so that our sins could be forgiven, then God raised Him from the dead, to reign as King of Kings and Lord of Lords! This is the hope that we have to celebrate in Advent and all year long! In the words of a very familiar Christmas carol, "Joy to the world, the LORD has come! Let Earth receive her King. Let every heart prepare Him room!" Let's make room for Jesus in this home, and we pray that each member of our family would make room for Him in your heart.

Family Activity

Jesus began His life in a manger and ended it on a cross. Many people believe that the manger might have been made of wood, so for this activity we are going to imagine Jesus starting His earthly life lying on hay in a wooden manger, then ending His life hanging on a wooden cross. We will make one special ornament to give us this visual picture. Using wooden craft sticks, take two and make a cross. Next, make a loop out of twine or ribbon and hang on your tree.

December 23

The Psalms are a very special group of passages, written mostly by David with many to be actually sung. We talked earlier of the importance that the Old Testament played in leading us to Jesus in the form of prophecy. Remember we rolled the dice or drew cards and tried to guess what number or card would be drawn? The Psalms are certainly filled with it. Prophecy is the prediction of something happening before it ever happens. However, here are some other special things we see pointing to Jesus, through the Psalms: The disciples who wrote parts of the Bible recited the Psalms, Jesus Himself quoted the Psalms, the Psalms lead us to a powerful way to worship God, the Psalms can be used as a prayer when we don't know what to pray, and finally, the Psalms tell us of the way Jesus came to redeem us from our sin, even though they were written well before Jesus was born.

Family Activity

When we think about David, we probably think about the fact that he was a shepherd. And when we think about Jesus, we probably remember that He is our Good Shepherd who lovingly leads us, and that He is our Savior who died in our place. Hold a candy cane in your hand. What shape is it? It's a shepherd's staff. What letter does it make? It makes the letter "J" for Jesus! What colors are on it? It's red for the blood He shed and white for His perfect life. Let's eat the candy and thank Jesus for being our Shepherd!

December 24

Christmas Eve—what a special day! And what a blessing it has been to spend time together studying God's Word! Over our days of study in the Old Testament, we have seen God make His plan to redeem the world very obvious! Sadly, though, many people live their entire lives and miss this truth. They don't miss it because God is keeping His great news from them, they miss it because they are not looking in the right places or are not willing to listen to the right message.

It is our highest hope and prayer that you will live your life with an overwhelming understanding that God is for you, He sent His son to redeem your life, and that you will live to spread this news to those in your world! As we wrap up study on how Jesus can be seen in the Old Testament, we want to make sure you understand the meaning of the Old Testament prophets. The Old Testament prophets were used by God to prepare the way for Jesus, and the prophets spoke words that came straight from God, not their own. In the little town of Bethlehem on a silent, holy night, the words of the prophets were fulfilled, and Christ our Savior was born!

Family Activity

Read together this wonderful passage which was prophesied in the book of Matthew: "Now the birth of Jesus Christ took place in this way. When his mother Mary had been engaged to Joseph, before they came together she was found to be with child from the Holy Spirit. Behold, an angel of the Lord appeared to him (Joseph) in a dream, saying, 'Joseph, son of David, do not fear to take Mary as your wife, for that which is conceived in her is from the Holy Spirit. She will bear a son, and you shall call his name Jesus, for he will save his people from their sins.' All this took place to fulfill what the Lord had spoken by the prophet: Behold, the virgin shall conceive and bear a son, and they shall call his name Immanuel" (Matthew 1:18-23).

Worship together at a Christmas Eve church service!

December 25

As we come to the close of this wonderful Advent season, let's fix our eyes on the second Advent of our Lord. Scripture tells us that he came once to redeem our sin, and He will come again to reign as King! As we celebrate the precious baby Jesus who was sent to save us, let us look forward with just as much anticipation to the second coming of our reigning King! As Christians, we can live each day with this hope-filled feeling of anticipation as we look forward to heaven. We can have peace in the midst of hard times, love for our brothers and sisters, and salvation from the sin that weighs us down—all because of the gift God gave us when He gave us Jesus. He is the very best Christmas present in the world! He is worth seeking with all of your heart and trusting for all of your life.

When Jesus left His disciples after He rose from the dead, He left them with this promise: "Do not let your hearts be troubled. Trust in God; trust also in me. In my Father's house are many rooms; if it were not so, I would have told you. I am going there to prepare a place for you. And if I go and prepare a place for you, I will come back and take you to be with me that you also may be where I am" (John 14:1-3).

As we have seen all through the Bible, God keeps His promises. He was faithful to fulfill His covenant when He sent His one and only Son to save all people who trust in Him. And He will be true to His promise to come back for us to conquer sin and death one last time. After that, His word promises a true community of people where there is no sickness, death or tears, no sin, struggle or fighting, only the true, perfect life we were created for with God in heaven forever! So today, as we celebrate Christmas day, may we not forget we have an even better day coming for us with Jesus!

Family Activity

Read the Christmas account in Luke 2 and make special memories together!

Meet Heather McAnear

Heather McAnear is from Oklahoma City and has called Council Road Baptist Church her church home for more than fifteen years. She and her husband, Garrick, enjoy teaching in the Adult Connection ministry and leading a Community Group in their home. They are also busy raising their three children and enjoy going on short-term mission trips. Heather loves to communicate God's truths in a practical way, through spoken and written words. This is her fourth family Bible study, and she was honored to partner with Pastor Rick on this project.

Endnotes

[1] Christian Smith, *Soul Searching, The Religious and Spiritual Lives of American Teenagers* (Oxford University Press, 2005).

[2] Kenda Creasy Dean, *Almost Christian, What the Faith of the American Teenager is Telling the Church* (Oxford University Press, 2010).

[3] J.B. Phillips, *Your God Is Too Small* (Touchstone Publishers, May 1, 1997).

[4] Christopher Wright, *Knowing Jesus through the Old Testament* (IVP Academic, 1992).

[5] Peter Stoner, *Bible Science* (Moody Press, 1958).

[6] Walter Kaiser, *The Case for Jesus the Messiah* (Melbourne: Pacific College Study Series, 1994), 17-18.

[7] Saint Athanasius, *On the Incarnation of the Word*, 129.

[8] Graeme Goldsworthy, *According to Plan* (Downers Grove, IL: IVP, 1991).

[9] Charles Spurgeon, *Sermon at Metropolitan Tabernacle, "Christ Precious to Believers"* (March 13, 1859. Spurgeon Archives).

[10] Richard Pratt, *He Gave Us Stories* (P&R Publishing, June 1, 1993).

[11] David Murray, *Jesus on Every Page* (Thomas Nelson Publishing, 2013).

[12] David Martin Lloyd Jones, *The Gospel in Genesis* (Crossway Publishing, 2009).

[13] Jonathan Edwards, *A History of the Work of Redemption* (Banner of Truth, 2003).

[14] David Murray, *Jesus on Every Page* (2013).

[15] Arno Penzias as quoted by Walter Bradley in "The Just So Universe" (LeadershipU.com archive, 1999).

[16] Patrick Fairbairn, *The Typology of Scripture* (Nabu Press, 2010).

[17] William Van Gemeran, *The Progress of Redemption* (Baker Book House, 2008).

[18] J.R.R. Tolkien, as quoted by Alistair McGrath.

[19] C.S. Lewis, as quoted by Alistair McGrath.

[20] Bryan Chappel, *Christ-Centered Preaching* (Baker Academic, 2005).

[21] John Bunyan, *Grace Abounding to the Chief of Sinners* (Hertfordshire: Evangelical Press 1978).

[22] F.F. Bruce, *New Testament Development of Old Testament Themes* (Wipf and Stock Publishers 2004).

[23] Jennifer Newton Tait, *John Newton, Slave Trader* (Christian History Magazine, August 8, 2008).

[24] Robert Walsh, *Aboard a Slave Ship* (Eye Witness to History, 2000).

[25] Tim Keller. Sermon at 2009, Together for the Gospel Conference.

[26] C.S. Lewis, *The Weight of Glory* (HarperOne Publishers, 2009).

[27] NIV Study Bible (Crossway Publishers, 2012).

[28] Charles Spurgeon. Sermon at Metropolitan Baptist Church London in 1904 titled, "David's First Victory."

[29] John Calvin. *Institutes* (Westminister Press, 1960).

[30] Charles Spurgeon, "The Rainbow". A sermon preached at Metropolitan Tabernacle on June 26, 1863.

[31] Genesis 15 and Exodus 12 indicate that the Israelites were in Egypt for over 400 years. So why do I say here that it was sixty years from Joseph to Moses? The answer is that the Scriptural account in those passages is not dated from the time of Joseph, but from the time of Abraham and his descendants. So the sojourns of Isaac and Ishmael into Egypt would have been included in that accounting. So the time between the Abrahamic promise and the time of Moses was 430 years. The exact time between the death of Joseph and the birth of Moses was sixty-seven years.

[32] John Piper. *God's Covenant with David: Desiring God* (Sermon Podcast; December 18, 1983).

[33] D.A. Carson, *A Call to Spiritual Reformation* (Baker Academic, June 1992).

[34] "Amy Winehouse Obituary" (*The Birmingham Mail*, July 13, 2011).

[35] I've heard the illustration of the fish in the fish bowl from two different preachers—Adrian Rogers and Tim Keller. My assumption is that it is, therefore, a commonly used analogy. I did, however, want to give proper credit.

[36] David Murray, *Jesus on Every Page* (2013).

[37] Excerpts from Martin Luther, *Treatise Concerning Good Works* (1520).

[38] John Piper, *How Christ Ended the Old Testament Regime* (Desiring God Sermon Archives, 2005).

[39] Philo of Alexandria, *On the Special Laws* (On the Decalogue, Loeb Classical Library, Chapter 1, Page 96).

[40] Dr. Derick Kidner (*The Tyndale Old Testament Commentary, Psalm 1-72*).

[41] Evelyn Underhill, *Worship* (2002).

[42] *Jesus on Every Page*

[43] Tim Keller, *The Reason for God: Belief in an Age of Skepticism* (Penguin Group, 2008).